Big White Ghetto

KEVIN D. WILLIAMSON

Big White Ghetto

Dead Broke, Stone-Cold Stupid, and High on Rage in the Dank Woolly Wilds of the "Real America"

REGNERY
PUBLISHING
A Division of Salem Media Group

Regnery® is a registered trademark of Salem Communications Holding Corporation

ISBN 978-1-62157-969-4
eISBN 978-1-62157-994-6
Library of Congress Control Number: 2020939343

Published in the United States by
Regnery Publishing
A Division of Salem Media Group
Washington, DC
www.Regnery.com

Manufactured in the United States of America

10 9 8 7 6 5 4 3 2

Books are available in quantity for promotional or premium use. For information on discounts and terms, please visit our website: www.Regnery.com.

For Jay Nordlinger, *il miglior fabbro.*

Contents

Big White Ghetto   1

White Trash Receptacle   15

I Am Cancer   29

"Boy"   35

The Weed Man Is All Up in the
Chamber of Commerce   51

The Wisenheimers of Cabrini-Green   61

Screaming Man   71

Play to Extinction   79

Topless Chick, Uncredited   89

Whose Streets?   101

Sunny California, Shady Russians   109

Der Apfelstrudelführers   117

Down and Out in R.A.T.T. Town   129

Death of a Fucking Salesman   139

Adventures in National Socialism   143

Farming Dirty   153

Among the Flat-Earthers   165

Pillars of Fire   171

In the Valley of the Giant Robots   181

The White Minstrel Show   195

Dead Broke and Stone-Cold Stupid in Paradise   207

Sinners in the Hands of an Indifferent God   215

Acknowledgments   219

Notes   223

Index   227

Big White Ghetto

Owsley County, Kentucky

THERE ARE LOTS OF DIVERSIONS IN THE BIG WHITE GHETTO, the vast moribund matrix of Wonder Bread–hued Appalachian towns and villages stretching from northern Mississippi to southern New York. It's a slowly dissipating nebula of poverty and misery with its heart in eastern Kentucky, the last redoubt of the Scots-Irish working class that picked up where African slave labor left off, mining and cropping and sawing the raw materials for a modern American economy that would soon run out of profitable uses for the class of people who five hundred years ago would have been known, without any derogation intended, as peasants. Thinking about the future here, with its bleak prospects, is not much fun at all. So instead of too much black-minded introspection you have the pills and the dope, the morning beers, the endless scratch-off lotto cards, the healing meetings up on the hill, the federally funded ritual of trading cases of food-stamp Pepsi for packs of Kentucky's Best cigarettes and good old hard currency, tall piles of gas-station nachos, the occasional blast of meth, Narcotics Anonymous meetings, petty crime, THE DRAW, the recreational making and surgical unmaking of teenaged mothers, and death: Life expectancies are short; the typical man here dies well over a decade earlier than a man in Fairfax

County, Virginia. And they are getting shorter, women's life expectancy having declined by nearly 1.1 percent from 1987 to 2007.

If the people here weren't 98.5 percent white, we'd call it a reservation.

Driving through these hills and hollows, you aren't in the Appalachia of Elmore Leonard's *Justified* or squatting with Lyndon Johnson on Tom Fletcher's front porch in Martin County, a scene famously photographed by Walter Bennett of *Time*, the image that launched the so-called War on Poverty. The music isn't "Shady Grove," it's *thumpa-thumpa-thumpa* Kanye West. There is still coal mining—which, at twenty-five dollars an hour or more, is one of the more desirable occupations outside of government work. But the jobs are moving west, and Harlan County, the heart of coal country, has lost nearly half of its population over the past thirty years.

There is here a strain of fervid and sometimes apocalyptic Christianity. Visions of the Rapture must have a certain appeal for people who already have been left behind. Like its black urban counterparts, the Big White Ghetto suffers from a whole trainload of social problems, but the most significant among them may be adverse selection: Those who have the required work skills, the academic ability, or the simple desperate native enterprising grit to do so get the hell out as fast as they can, and they have been doing that for decades. As they go businesses disappear, institutions fall into decline, social networks erode, and there is little or nothing left over for those who remain. It's a classic economic death spiral: The quality of the available jobs is not enough to keep good workers, and the quality of the available workers is not enough to attract good jobs. These little towns located at remote wide spots in helical mountain roads are hard enough to get to if you have a good reason to be here. If you don't have a good reason, you aren't going to think of one.

Appalachian places have evocative and unsentimental names denoting deep roots: Little Barren River, Coal Pit Road. The name "Cumberland" blankets Appalachian geography—the Cumberland Mountains, the Cumberland River, several Cumberland counties—in tribute to the

Duke of Cumberland, who along with the Ulster Scots ancestors of the Appalachian settlers crushed the Young Pretender at the Battle of Culloden. Even church names suggest ancient grievances: SEPARATE Baptist, with the descriptor in all-capital letters. ("Come out from among them and be ye separate" [2 Corinthians 6:17].) I pass a church called "Welfare Baptist," which, unfortunately, describes much of the population for miles and miles around.

THERE IS NOT MUCH NOVELTY IN BOONEVILLE, KENTUCKY, the seat of Owsley County, but it does receive a steady trickle of visitors: Its public figures suffer politely through a perverse brand of tourism from journalists and do-gooders every time the U.S. Census data are recalculated and it defends its dubious title as poorest county in these United States.[1] The first person I encounter is Jimmy—I think he's called Jimmy; there is so much alcohol and Kentucky in his voice that I have a hard time understanding him—who is hanging out by the steps of the local municipal building waiting for something to happen, and what happens today is me. Unprompted, he breaks away from the little knot of men he is standing with and comes at me smiling hard. He appears to be one of those committed dipsomaniacs of the sort David Foster Wallace had in mind when he observed that at a certain point in a drunk's career it does not matter all that much whether he's actually been drinking, that's just the way he is. Jimmy is attached to one of the clusters of unbusy men who lounge in front of the public buildings in Booneville —"old timers with nothing to do," one observer calls them, though some of those "old-timers" do not appear to have reached thirty yet, and while their Mossy Oak camouflage outfits say "Remington," their complexions say "Nintendo." Mossy Oak and Realtree camo are aesthetic touchstones in these parts: I spot a new $50,000 Ram pickup truck with an exterior as shiny as a silver ingot and a camouflage interior, the utility of which is not obvious.

I expect Jimmy to ask for money, but instead he launches into a long disquisition about something called the "Thread the Needle" program, relating with great animation how he convinced a lady acquaintance of his to go down to the county building and offer to sign up for Thread the Needle, telling her that she would receive twenty-five or fifty dollars for doing so.

"'THREAD THE NEEDLE!' I TOLD HER," he says. "RIGHT? RIGHT?" He pantomimes threading a needle. He laughs. I don't quite get it. So he tells the story again in what I assume are more or less the exact same slurred words. "RIGHT?"

"Right . . ."

"But they ain't no Thread the Needle program! I play pranks!"

I get it: Advising friends to go down to the county building to sign up for imaginary welfare programs is Jimmy's personal entertainment. He's too old for World of Warcraft and too drunk for the Shoutin' Happy Mission Ministry.

It's not like he has a lot of appealing options, though. There used to be two movie theaters here—a regular cinema and a drive-in. Both are long gone. The nearest Walmart is nearly an hour away. There's no bookstore, the nearest Barnes & Noble being fifty-five miles away and the main source of reading matter being the horrifying-hilarious crime blotter in the local weekly newspaper. Within living memory, this town had three grocery stores, a Western Auto and a NAPA Auto Parts, a feed store, a lumber store, a clothing shop, a Chrysler dealership, a used-car dealership, a skating rink—even a discotheque back in the 1970s. Today there is one grocery store, and the rest is as dead as disco. If you want a newsstand or a dinner at Applebee's, gas up the car. Amazon may help, but delivery can be tricky—the nearest UPS drop box is seventeen miles away, the nearest FedEx office thirty-four miles away.

If you go looking for the catastrophe that laid this area low, you'll eventually discover a terrifying reality: *Nothing happened.* It's not like this was a company town and the business around which life was organized went tits-up. Booneville and Owsley County were never economic powerhouses. They were sustained for a time in part by a nearby Midsouth plant, which manufactured consumer electronics such as steam irons and toaster ovens, as well as industrial supplies such as refrigerator parts. A former employee estimates that a majority of Owsley County households owed part of their income to Midsouth at one time or another, until a mishap in the sanding room put an end to that: "Those shavings are just like coal dust," he says. "It will go right up if it gets a spark." Operations were consolidated in a different facility, a familiar refrain here—a local branch of the health department consolidated operations in a different town, along with the energy company and others. But Owsley County was poor before, during, and after that period. Coal mining was for years a bulwark against utter economic ruination, but regulation, a lengthy permitting process, and other factors both economic and geological pushed what remains of the region's coal business away toward other communities. After they spend a winter or two driving an hour or two each way over icy twists of unforgiving mountain asphalt, many locals working in the coal business decide it is easier to move to where the work is, leaving Owsley County, where unemployment is already 150 percent of the national average, a little more desperate and collectively jobless than before. It's possible that a coal worker's moving from Booneville to Pikeville would lower the median income of both towns.

Some hope that a long-awaited highway improvement program will revitalize the town by making the drive a little less terrifying—the local police chief admits with some chagrin that he recently found himself heading down the road in panicked spins after encountering a patch of early-November black ice, which clings to the low and shady places. But the fact is, KY-30 is a two-way road, and there are still more reasons to leave Owsley County than to go there.

A few locals drive two hours—on a good day, more on a bad one—to report for work in the Toyota factory at Georgetown, Kentucky, which means driving all the way through the Daniel Boone National Forest and greater Lexington to reach the suburbs on the far side. As with the coal miners traveling past Hazard or even farther, eventually many of those Toyota workers decide they might as well live where their jobs are. The employed and upwardly mobile leave, taking their children, their capital, and their habits with them, clean clear of the Big White Ghetto, while the unemployed, the dependent, and the addicted are once again left behind.

"We worked before," the former Midsouth man says. "We'd work again."

"WELL, *YOU* TRY PAYING THAT MUCH FOR A CASE OF POP!" says the irritated proprietor of a nearby café, who is curt with whoever is on the other end of the telephone but greets customers with the perfect manners that small town restaurateurs reliably develop. I don't think much of that overheard remark at the time, but it turns out that the local economy runs on black-market soda the way Baghdad ran on contraband crude during the days of Saddam Hussein and sanctions.

It works like this: Once a month, the debit card accounts of those receiving what we still call "food stamps" are credited with a few hundred dollars—about $500 for a family of four, on average—which are immediately converted into a unit of exchange, in this case cases of soda. On the day the accounts are credited, local establishments accepting EBT cards—and all across the Big White Ghetto, "WE ACCEPT FOOD STAMPS" is the new *E pluribus unum*—are swamped with locals using their public benefits to buy cases and cases of soda; reports put the number at thirty to forty cases for some buyers. Those cases of soda then either go on to another retailer, who buys them at 50 cents on the dollar, in effect laundering those $500 in monthly benefits into $250 in cash—a considerably worse rate than your typical organized-crime money launderer offers—or else they go into the local black-market economy, where they can be used as currency in such ventures as the dealing of unauthorized prescription painkillers—by "pillbillies," as they are known at the sympathetic establishments in Florida that do so much business with Kentucky and West Virginia that the relevant interstate bus service is nicknamed the "OxyContin Express." A woman who is intimately familiar with the local drug economy suggests that the exchange rate between sexual favors and cases of pop—some dealers will accept either—is about 1:1, meaning that the value of a woman in the local prescription-drug economy is about $12.99 at Walmart prices.

Last year, eighteen big-city mayors, Mike Bloomberg and Rahm Emanuel among them, sent the federal government a letter asking that soda be removed from the list of items eligible to be used for EBT purchases. Mayor Bloomberg delivered his standard sermon about obesity, nutrition, and the multiplex horrors of sugary drinks. But none of those mayors gets what's really going on with sugar water and food stamps. Take soda off the list and there will be another fungible commodity to take its place. It's possible that a great many cans of soda used as currency go a long time without ever being cracked—in a town this small, those selling soda to EBT users and those buying it back at half price are bound to be some of the same people, the soda merely changing hands ceremonially to mark the real exchange of value—pillbilly wampum.

"OH, WE'S JES' POOOOOR FOLLLLLKS, WE CAIN'T AFFORD NO CORN-BREAAAAAAAD!" So says Booneville police chief Johnny Logsdon, who has an amused glint in his eye and has encountered his share of parachuted-in writers on the poverty beat. A former New York City resident who made his career in the U.S. Navy before following his wife back to her old Kentucky home, Chief Logsdon is an outdoorsman and a gifted nature photographer (his work adorns the exterior of the municipal building) who speaks fondly of Staten Island but is clearly in his element in the Kentucky countryside, much of which is arrestingly beautiful.

Chief Logsdon has time to indulge his hobbies because the Big White Ghetto is different from most other ghettos in one very important way: There's not much violent crime here. There's a bit of the usual enterprise one finds everywhere there are drugs and poor people, which is to say, everywhere: Police have just broken up a ring of car burglars who had the inspired idea of pulling off their capers during Sunday-morning church services, when all the good people were otherwise occupied. (The good people? One victim reported $1,000 in cash missing from the trunk of his car, and I'm putting an asterisk next to his name until I know where that came from.) But even the crime here is pretty well predictable. The chief's assistant notes that if they know the nature and location of a particular crime, they can more or less drive straight to where the perpetrator, who is likely to be known to them intimately, is to be found. In Owsley County, "the usual suspects" is something more than a figure of speech.

There's a great deal of drug use, welfare fraud, and the like, but the overall crime rate throughout Appalachia is about two-thirds the national average, and the rate of violent crime is half the national average, according to the National Criminal Justice Reference Service. Chief Logsdon is justifiably skeptical of the area's reputation for drug-fueled crime. But he is not blinkered, and his photos of spectacular autumn foliage and delicate baby birds do not denote a sentimental disposition. "We have loggers and coal producers," he says, dropping the cornpone accent. "We have educators and local businesses, and people in the arts. And we have the same problems they have in every community." He points out that Booneville recently opened up a $1 million public library—a substantial investment for a town in which the value of all residential property combined would not add up to the big lottery jackpot being advertised all over. (Lottery tickets, particularly the scratch-off variety, are ubiquitous here.) He does not deny the severity or scope of the region's problems, but he does think that they are exaggerated by visitors who are here, after all, only because Owsley holds the national title for poorest county. Owsley's dependent underclass has many of the same problems as any other dependent underclass; but with a poverty rate persistently at the 40 percent mark—or half again as much poverty as in the Bronx—the underclass plays an outsized role in local life. It is not the exception.

Two towns over, I ask a young woman about the local gossip, and she tells me it's always the same: "Who's growing weed, who's not growing weed anymore, who's cooking meth, whose meth lab got broken into, whose meth lab blew up." Chief Logsdon thinks I may be talking to the wrong people. "Maybe that's all they see, because that's all they know.

Ask somebody else and they'll tell you a different story." He then gives me a half-joking—but only half—list of people not to talk to: not the shiftless fellows milling about in the hallways on various government-related errands, not the guy circling the block on a moped. Instead, there's the lifelong banker whose brother is the head of the school board. There's the mayor, a sharp nonagenarian who has been in office since the Eisenhower administration.

And that, too, is part of the problem with adverse selection in the Big White Ghetto: For the smart and enterprising people left behind, life can be very comfortable, with family close, a low cost of living, beautiful scenery, and a very short climb to the top of the social pecking order. The relative ease of life for the well-off and connected here makes it easy to overlook the real unpleasant facts of economic life, which helps explain why Booneville has a lovely new golf course, of all things, but so little in the way of everyday necessities. The county seat, run down as parts of it are, is an outpost of civilization compared with what surrounds it for fifty miles in every direction. Stopping for gas on KY-30 a few miles past the Owsley County line, I go looking for the restroom and discover instead that the family operating the place is living in makeshift quarters in the back. Margaret Thatcher lived above her family's shop as a little girl, too, but a grocer's in Grantham is a very different thing from a gas station in Kentucky, with very different prospects.

Owsley County had been dry since Prohibition. A close election (632–518) earlier this year changed that, and the local authorities are sorting out the regulatory and licensing issues related to the sale of alcohol. Chief Logsdon thinks that this is, on balance, a good thing, because local prohibition meant that local drunks were on the local roads coming back from bars or liquor stores. "They aren't waiting until they get home," he says. "They're opening the bottle. They're like kids at Christmas." Obviously, prohibition wasn't getting the job done. At the same time, the scene in Owsley County might make even the most ardent libertarian think twice about drug legalization: After all, these addicts are hooked on legal drugs—OxyContin and other prescription opioid analgesics—even if they often are obtained illegally. In nearby Whitley County, nearly half of the examined inmates in one recent screening tested positive for buprenorphine, also known as "prison heroin," a product originally developed as a treatment for opiate addiction. (Such cures are often worse than the disease: Bayer once owned the trademark on heroin, which it marketed as a cure for morphine addiction—it works.) Fewer drunk drivers would be a good thing, but I have to imagine that the local bar, if Booneville ever gets one, is going to be a grim place.

THIS ISN'T THE KENTUCKY OF ELMORE LEONARD'S IMAGINATION, and there is nothing romantic about it. These are no sons and daughters of Andrew Jackson, no fiercely independent remnants of the old America clinging to their homes and their traditional ways. Having once been downwind of a plate of biscuits and squirrel gravy does not make you Daniel Boone. This is not the land of moonshine and hill lore, but of families of four clutching $40 worth of lotto scratchers and crushing the springs on their beaten-down Camry while getting dinner from a Phillips 66 station.

This is about "THE DRAW."

"THE DRAW," the monthly welfare checks that supplement dependents' earnings in the black-market Pepsi economy, is poison. It's a potent enough poison to catch the attention even of such people as write for the *New York Times*. Nicholas Kristof, visiting nearby Jackson, Kentucky, last year, was shocked by parents who were taking their children out of literacy classes because improved academic performance would threaten $700-a-month Social Security disability benefits, which increasingly are paid out for nebulous afflictions such as loosely defined learning disorders. "This is painful for a liberal to admit," Kristof wrote, "but conservatives have a point when they suggest that America's safety net can sometimes entangle people in a soul-crushing dependency."

There is much here to confound conservatives, too. Jim DeMint likes to say that marriage is our best anti-poverty program, and he also has a point. But a 2004 study found that the majority of impoverished households in Appalachia were headed by married couples, not single mothers. Getting and staying married is not a surefire prophylactic against poverty. Neither are prophylactics. Kentucky has a higher teen motherhood rate than the national average, but not radically so, and its young mothers are more likely to be married. Kentucky is number nineteen in the ranking of states by teen pregnancy rates, but it is number eight when it comes to teen birth rates, according to the Guttmacher Institute, its young women being somewhat less savage than most of their counterparts across the country. Kentucky and West Virginia have abortion rates that are one-fourth those of Rhode Island or Connecticut, and one-fifth that of Florida. More marriage, less abortion: not exactly the sort of thing out of which conservative indictments are made. But marriage is less economically valuable, at least to men, in Appalachia—like their counterparts elsewhere, married men here earn more than their unmarried counterparts, but the difference is smaller and declining.

In effect, welfare has made Appalachia into a big and sparsely populated housing project—too backward to thrive, but just comfortable enough to keep the underclass in place. There is no cure for poverty, because there is no cause of poverty—poverty is the natural condition of the human animal. It is not as though labor and enterprise are unknown here: Digging coal is hard work, farming is hard work, timbering is hard work—so hard that the best and brightest long ago packed up for Cincinnati or Pittsburgh or Memphis or Houston. There is to this day an Appalachian bar in Detroit and ex-Appalachian enclaves around the country. The lesson of the Big White Ghetto is the same as the lessons we learned about the urban housing projects in the late twentieth century: The best public policy treatment we have for poverty is dilution. But like the old project towers, the Appalachian draw culture produces concentration, a socioeconomic Salton Sea that becomes more toxic every year.

"The government gives people checks, but nobody teaches them how to live," says Teresa Barrett, a former high school principal who now publishes the Owsley County newspaper. "You have people on the draw getting $3,000 a month, and they still can't live. When I was at the school, we'd see kids come in from a long weekend just starved to death. But you'll see those parents at the grocery store with their fifteen cases of Pepsi, and that's all they've got in the buggy—you know what they're doing. Everybody knows, nobody does anything. And when you have that many people on the draw, that's a big majority of voters."

Her advice to young people is to study for degrees that will help them get jobs in the schools or at the local nursing home—or get out. "I would move in a heartbeat," she says, but she stays for family reasons.

Speaking in the Rose Garden in March 1965, Lyndon Johnson had high hopes for his Appalachia Bill. "This legislation marks the end of an era of partisan cynicism towards human want and misery. The dole is dead. The pork barrel is gone. Federal and state, liberal and conservative, Democrat and Republican, Americans of these times are concerned with the outcome of the next generation, not the next election. . . . The bill that I will now sign will work no miracles overnight. Whether it works at all depends not upon the federal government alone but the states and the local governments as well." The dole, as it turns out, is deathless, and the pork barrel has merely been reincarnated as a case of Pepsi. President Johnson left out of his calculations the factor that the populists almost always overlook: the people.

Owsley County went 83.8 percent for Donald Trump in the 2016 election.

There is another Booneville, this one in northern Mississippi, just within the cultural orbit of Memphis and a stone's throw from the two-room shack in which was born Elvis Presley, the Appalachian Adonis. There's a lot of Big White Ghetto between them, trailers and rickety homes heated with wood stoves, the post-industrial ruins of old mills and small factories with their hard 1970s lines that always make me think of the name of the German musical group Einstürzende Neubauten—"collapsing modern buildings." (Some things just sound more appropriate in German.) You swerve to miss deer on the country roads, see the rusted hulk of a

1937 Dodge sedan nestled against a house, and wonder if somebody was once planning to restore it—or if somebody just left it there on his way to Detroit. You see the clichés: cars up on cinder blocks, to be sure, but houses up on cinder blocks, too. And you get a sense of the enduring isolation of some of these little communities: About twenty miles from Williamsburg, Kentucky, I become suspicious that I have not selected the easiest route to get where I'm going, and stop and ask a woman what the easiest way to get to Williamsburg is. "You're a hell of a long way from Virginia," she answers. I tell her I'm looking for Williamsburg, Kentucky, and she says she's never heard of it. It's about the third town over, the nearest settlement of any interest, and it's where you get on the interstate to go up to Lexington or down to Knoxville. "I went to Hazard once," she offers. The local economic-development authorities say that the answer to Appalachia's problems is sending more people to college. Sending them to Nashville might be a start.

Eventually, I find my road. You run out of Big White Ghetto pretty quickly, and soon you are among the splendid farms and tall straight trees of northern Mississippi. Appalachia pretty well fades away after Tupelo, and the Mississippi River begins to assert its cultural force. Memphis is only a half-hour's drive away, but it feels like a different sort of civilization—another ghetto, but a ghetto of a different sort. And if you stand in front of the First Baptist Church on Beale Street and look over your shoulder back toward the mountains, you don't see the ghost of Elvis or Devil Anse or Daniel Boone—you see a big sign that says "WONDER BREAD," cheap and white and empty and as good an epitaph as any for what remains left behind in those hills and hollows, waiting on the draw and trying not to think too hard about what the real odds are on the lotto or an early death.

White Trash Receptacle

Lubbock, Texas

THERE IS A PROVERB sometimes attributed to Confucius: "To put the nation in order, we must first put the family in order." Half-assed Confucianism can be powerful stuff, and Anthony Kennedy cited the Chinese sage—"Confucius taught that marriage lies at the foundation of government"—in his *Obergefell* gay-marriage decision, which did not put the family in order but rather achieved the opposite.

The idea is common in other schools of philosophy: For the Stoics, familial love (as opposed to dangerous, free-ranging *eros*) was the model for social relations. We speak of "the father of the country," a title (*pater patriae*) given by the Romans first to a victorious general, Camillus, whom they regarded as the architect of Rome's "second founding" after the Gallic siege, then to Cicero after his exposure of Catiline's plot to overthrow the government, and then to Julius Caesar, after which it became a commonplace on the litany of imperial titles. Aristotle warned us not to make too much of the paternal metaphor: "Some suppose that statesman, king, estate manager, and master of a family have a common character. This is a mistake; they think that the distinction between them is not a difference in kind, but a simple, numerical difference." That advice has seldom been heeded: The English word "economy" comes from the Greek word for household husbandry (οἰκονομία), and even in the early days of the twenty-first century we have not emancipated ourselves from the superstition that the president—our national dad, as Governor John Kasich insists—manages the economy like a salaryman who sits down once a month to write checks and go over the bills. We think about the president in much the same way as primitives thought about their priest-kings, sacrificing them when the rains don't come and the crops fail.

The distastefully squishy left-wing social theorist George Lakoff argues that the Right sees the nation as needing strict, patriarchal family structure, while the Left advocates a nurturing, maternal national family. But the president isn't our father, and the nation isn't a family. The belief that the nation is a family that ought to be governed by a father-analogue is what separates nationalism from conservatism, which in the Anglo-American context is deeply rooted in the classical-liberal philosophy of the American founding. Blood-and-soil, throne-and-altar nationalism is a very large part of conservatism in the European context, and in the context of many backward countries and political movements ranging from the Marathi-chauvinist Shiv Sena in India to North Korea's *juche* to the *uyoku dantai* in Japan. But every metaphor points in two directions: Nationalism is not only a sentimental veneer for political movements that are generally corrupt and authoritarian—nationalism is also a lament for the idealized family that never existed, the loss of which is nonetheless felt acutely.

But I do not wish to dwell too long among these abstractions. Instead, I want to write about Michael. And, as Captain Willard tells us in *Apocalypse Now*: "There is no way to tell his story without telling my own."

MICHAEL BRENDAN DOUGHERTY IS BITTER. I think that I can write that in both truth and charity. (I think you might even say that he and I are friends.) Dougherty is a conservative of the sort sometimes advertised as "paleo," and served as national correspondent for the

American Conservative.[1] Like many conservative writers with those associations, Dougherty spends a great deal of time lambasting the conservative movement and its organs, from which he feels, for whatever reason, estranged—an alienation that carries with it more than a little suggestion that it is somewhat personal. In 2013, he announced that he planned to set aside political writing to concentrate on the relatively sane world of professional baseball, saying: "National politics has most of the vices of 'bread and circuses.' And if that's the case, pro sports is a better circus." But it is difficult for a politics man to give up politics—look at all the political crap that ESPN viewers and *Sports Illustrated* readers have to endure—and in this election cycle he has taken it upon himself to serve as Apostle to the Cathedral, "the Cathedral" being a favorite name of the so-called alt-right for the "distributed conspiracy" (in the words of Curtis Yarvin, a.k.a. Mencius Moldbug) that might in less riled-up times be described as "polite society," the conventional wisdom among people who live in places such as Washington and New York City and work in fields such as politics and media. You know: THEM. Explaining the benighted white working class to THEM is the cause, and sanctimony is the literary mode—for Dougherty, and for many others doing the same work with less grace.

Doughtery invites us to think about "Mike," an imaginary member of the white working class who is getting by on Social Security Disability fraud in unfashionable Garbutt, New York. In Dougherty's view, conservatives don't give a damn about Mike. On the other hand, they care a great deal about Jeffrey, "a typical coke-sniffer in Westport, Connecticut." Jeffrey pays a lot of taxes, both direct taxes in the form of the capital gains tax and indirectly through the corporate tax, and tax cuts "intersect with his interests at several points." Republicans want to encourage private retirement investments, which might send some business to Jeffrey's "fund-manager in-law, who works in nearby Darien." (For those of you unfamiliar with the econogeography of Fairfield County, Connecticut, going from Westport to Darien is moving up in the world. Next stop: Greenwich.) "If the conservative movement has any advice for Mike, it's to move out of Garbutt and maybe 'learn computers,'" Dougherty writes. "Any investments he made in himself previously are for naught. People rooted in their hometowns? That sentimentalism is for effete readers of Edmund Burke. Join the hyper-mobile world." Dougherty's piece is headlined "How Conservative Elites Disdain Working-Class Republicans," and I suppose I should mention that my own writing on the white working class's infatuation with Donald Trump is Exhibit A in Dougherty's case.

Never mind the petty sneering (as though the conservative movement consisted of septuagenarians who say things like "learn computers") and the apparent need to invent moral debasement (tax cuts are good for the rich people in Connecticut who don't use cocaine, too), and the disregard for those capital-driven parts of the economy that are outside of the Manhattan-Connecticut finance corridor. And never mind the math, either: It is really quite difficult to design tax cuts that benefit people who do not pay much in the way of federal taxes. Set all that aside: What, really, is the case for staying in Garbutt?

There was no Garbutt, New York, until 1804, when Zachariah Garbutt and his son, John, settled there. They built a grist mill, and in the course of digging its foundations they discovered a rich vein of gypsum, then used as a fertilizer. A gypsum industry sprang up and ran its course. Then Garbutt died. "As the years passed away, a change came over the spirit of their dream," wrote local historian George E. Slocum. "Their church was demolished and its timber put to an ignoble use; their schools were reduced to one, and that a primary; their hotels were converted into dwelling houses; their workshops, one by one, slowly and silently sank from sight until there was but little left to the burg except its name."

Slocum wrote that in . . . 1908.

The emergence of the gypsum-hungry wallboard industry gave Garbutt a little bump at the beginning of the twentieth century, but it wasn't enough. The U.S. Census Bureau doesn't even keep data on Garbutt. To invoke Burkean conservatism in the service of preserving a community that was exnihilated into existence around a single commodity and lasted barely a century is to indulge absurd sentimentality. Yes, young men of Garbutt—get off your asses and go find a job.

Stonehenge didn't work out, either: Good luck.

I SUPPOSE LUBBOCK, TEXAS, is a thriving cosmopolis compared with Garbutt, New York. It didn't feel that way growing up there. It isn't so much that Lubbock is small (it's bigger than Birmingham or Orlando), but it is remote: five hours to Dallas or Albuquerque, eight or nine hours to Houston or Denver. Unless you are attached to Texas Tech University, a medical practice, or government, there is not a great deal of economic opportunity, partly because of secular economic conditions, partly because of a hidebound local culture that emphasizes waiting one's turn, which may be a Burkean virtue in theory but in practice means waiting for somebody to die before you get a promotion. I myself left when the gentlemen scholars of the *Lubbock Avalanche-Journal* declined even to interview me (a copy editor at the time) for a job writing op-eds. And there wouldn't have been any point in interviewing me: They knew who they were going to hire, and had known for years. Law firms, banks, and other businesses work much the same way. Lubbock is home to what Republicans like to call "rock-ribbed conservatives"—70 percent of the voters pulled the R lever in the last presidential election, far higher than the Texas average—but it is a city kept alive almost exclusively by welfare: subsidies for the surrounding cotton farmers, state and federal money pouring into the university, and so forth. Business? My balcony in the city's sole high-rise apartment (you could live pretty high in Lubbock on eleven dollars an hour) faced a wind turbine and, in the distance, a dog-food plant.

Lubbock has the thing that most terrifies the Trump-voting white working class: Mexicans, and lots of them. More than a third of the county's population is Hispanic. (Those Hispanics are overwhelmingly Mexican in origin, but not exclusively. Some years back I was having lunch at an establishment outside of town frequented by farmworkers when the proprietor, about whose legal status in these United States I had some doubt, opined that we really needed to get control of the border. I pressed him. "Salvadorans," he said. "We can't let them in here.") There are billboards and business signs in Spanish and parts of town where Spanish seems to be heard more often than English. That isn't a new thing—not for West Texas—and it doesn't seem to be much of a big thing, either. College students who would never think about moving into a poor black neighborhood have lived in poor Hispanic neighborhoods around Texas Tech University for years. An Anglo-Hispanic romance is not remarked upon the way a white-black relationship still would be. Only 6 percent of the population are foreign-born, but 22 percent speak a language other than English at home. Some of that is Vietnamese or Bengali, but it's mostly Spanish.

Lubbock also has a lot of what's killing the poor white people: prescription-drug addiction and the heroin that follows on its coattails, meth, alcohol abuse, venereal disease, and so on. It is a college town in which barely a quarter of the adults have a bachelor's degree and nearly a fifth of the population lives in poverty.

There are a great many Mikes there. I did not know many Jeffreys.

Texas may be Ted Cruz's home turf, but Lubbock is in many ways Trump country. *Wonkblog* compared the counties Trump won in the so-called Super Tuesday primary with the demographic data and found trends that will surprise no one who has been paying attention. Life expectancies among non-college-educated white Americans have been collapsing in an almost unprecedented fashion, a trend not seen on such a large scale since the collapse of the Soviet Union and the social anarchy that prevailed in Russia afterward. Trump counties had proportionally fewer people with college degrees. Trump counties had fewer people working. And the white people in Trump counties were likely to die younger. The causes of death were "increased rates of disease and ill health, increased drug overdose and abuse, and suicide," *Wonkblog* reported.

This is horrifyingly consistent with other findings.

BY SOME ESTIMATES, American men's real (inflation-adjusted) earnings peaked in or around 1973—right around the time I was born, in fact. (My timing has always sucked.) American household incomes have continued to rise, thanks in no small part to the entry of more women into the workforce.

As I (and others more able) have argued at some length, the immediate postwar era, during which such economic powerhouses as Germany, the United Kingdom, and Japan were temporarily sidelined (having been burnt to the ground), was an unusual period for the United States. Having emerged from the war with our domestic industrial infrastructure largely unscathed and the field being temporarily cleared of competitors, we romped about the world economy for several decades—until the Europeans and the Japanese began to catch up. (Stein's Law: "If something cannot go on forever, it will stop.") We might have done almost anything during that period; what we decided to do was build a giant, corrupt welfare state, with Lyndon Johnson supplementing Franklin Roosevelt's New Deal with innovations such as Medicare and Medicaid.

These and other government adventures at all levels have proven ineffective and extraordinarily expensive, resulting in massive misallocations of capital that have left the United States less wealthy than it should be.

This is not to pick a fight with Paul Krugman about "competitiveness"—there was no regime, no matter how liberal, that was going to preserve our postwar hegemony—but rather to provide context for the fact that the American economy has thrived in ways that are not widely appreciated: We manufacture more today, radically more, in real terms than we did in the 1950s or 1980s. Our standard of living is much, much higher. There is poverty, and there is economic frustration, but what ails Donald Trump's America is not mainly material.

The wave of social change that forever changed American life in the postwar era—taking a turn for the disastrous—wasn't the influx of cheap electronics from Japan or the migration of some low-skilled jobs to places such as Taiwan and Hong Kong and then to mainland China.

It was divorce. It was the end of the American family as we had known it.

The manufacturing numbers—and the entire gloriously complex tale of globalization—go in fits and starts: A little improvement here, a little improvement there, and a radically better world in raw material terms every couple of decades. Go back and read the novels of the 1980s or watch *The Brady Bunch* and ask yourself why well-to-do suburban families living in large, comfortable homes and holding down prestigious jobs were worried about the price of meat—and try to remember the last time you heard someone complain that they couldn't afford a stick of butter, the price of which provided a small bit of characterization in Stephen King's *The Stand*, published in 1978. Do you know anybody who can't afford a stick of butter in 2020?

That change happened a little at a time, here and there.

The family-life numbers, on the other hand, came down on us like a meteor. Before the war, divorce was such an alien phenomenon that it animated shaggy-dog stories like *The Gay Divorcee*, a play in which a fictitious act of adultery had to be invented to move the plot forward. Divorce in 1960 was so rare as to carry a hint of scandalous glamour, the memory of which was kept alive through the 1970s and 1980s in magazine lifestyle articles about informal patio dinner parties for divorcées (a word faintly ludicrous today) in women's magazines, and men's magazines celebrating divorce as a second adolescence.

The divorce rate doubled over the span of a few decades—even as the marriage rate was declining. Add to that the violence of abortion, which fundamentally alters the relationships between men, women, and children, and what exactly "family" means to those of us born around the time *Roe v. Wade* was decided becomes a very difficult question.

I HAD THOUGHT THAT THE FIRE would finally do it. I was wrong.

My mother's second husband (of four) was a Vietnam veteran and one of those alcoholics who like to keep meticulous track of their alcohol intake. His drink at the time was Coors Light, and as he worked his way through a case of beer, he stacked his Silver Bullets in a neat little pyramid. He was a man who was very careful about some things: I've never seen anyone take such obsessively good care of a lawn mower, disassembling, cleaning, and lubricating it after every use. In other things, he was less careful: When he ran out of beer, he'd turn to anything in the house that had alcohol in it, or a suggestion of alcohol in it, including the 70-proof Mexican vanilla that my mother bought by the liter on trips to Juarez. That was strange: The scraggly, unshaved, cruel drunk sitting at the kitchen table—a man who'd kicked my head half in once when I was in first grade—smelled pleasantly of baked goods.

Of course there was violence. How could there not be? He had been living with us for some time (he lived in our house for a period when I, age six, had been turned out of it to divide my time between the homes of neighbors who took me in—evenings with one, mornings with another) and had proposed marriage to my mother on a Christmas morning when he, a delivery van driver, had neglected to buy her a Christmas present. She wept with joy at his proposal. I was skeptical.

She was, as is common, both a victim of violence and a perpetuator of it, a fact that some years later would have terrible consequences for a stepdaughter. She was obese, scarred, and partly paralyzed from a series of skin grafts necessitated by a horrible infection resulting from a scratch from her beloved poodle, Pepe. But she could still get in a few pretty good licks, especially when he was drunk to the point of near unconsciousness, which was pretty much all the time.

We were poor, of course, poor enough to be occasionally hungry. My mother worked, for a time, for a bill collector, which was hatefully ironic: We would shut the curtains and sit very quietly on the gold 1970s shag carpet when bill collectors came to our own door, and there were occasional days without electricity. One evening, just after dark, our doorbell rang and there was no one there when we answered—but there were a dozen sacks of groceries. Video games were a big thing at the time, and we would go to Furr's Supermarket to play *Defender* and *Scrambler* on those occasions when we were fortunate enough to have a quarter. (I know this sounds like walking to school in the snow, uphill both ways, but these are the facts.) On the other hand, there always was money for the *real* essentials: cable television (we even had HBO!) and cigarettes. Those were different times: My mother would send me, a small child, to the grocery store to buy cartons of cigarettes, which I purchased, paying by *check* before toddling off on my little bicycle. Nobody seemed to think this remarkable.

The cigarettes were the relevant item on this particular evening, though, because both members of the couple smoked enthusiastically (my mother's third husband smoked unfiltered Pall Malls *in his sleep*; you had to see it) and did so while doing other things: eating, stacking Coors Light cans, washing dishes, and so forth. They also sometimes smoked while they fought pitched battles in the living room, which was the case this evening. Somebody—my memory is a little fuzzy, but I believe it was him—went down on the hideous 1973 floral sofa, which, being made mainly of polyester, went up in flames. There were screams (hers) and my brother and I ran out of the house. (We were *laughing*.) She followed, with him in enraged pursuit. My brother and I sheltered in the next-door neighbor's garage while they fought it out in the front yard, right there on Fifty-Sixth Street in front of God and everybody, within shouting distance of the Second Baptist Church. She put some sort of James Bond judo hip-throw maneuver on him, pretty impressive for a woman with a partly paralyzed right arm, and he went ass over teakettle just before the police arrived.

Of course I got to ride along when we went to pick him up from jail. Of course I got to sit in the jailhouse and watch the drama unfold, just as I had been dragged along to Al-Anon meetings to play in the gravel parking lots of whatever church or community center was hosting these sad sacks while they assailed one another with tearful recriminations and promises of NEVER AGAIN. In a rare display of self-awareness, she made him lie down on the floorboard of our Volkswagen until the garage door was closed behind us, ashamed for the neighbors to see that she was taking him back. We were THOSE PEOPLE in a neighborhood whose crowning theatrical moment would be the funeral of a notorious motor-cycle-gang president at the home of his parents across the street, two very decent and kind people.

I was what you might call lightly attached to these miscreants. My mother was one-half of a couple who had adopted me late in life (I was born to a girl in her early teens whom I have not met, a trimester before *Roe v. Wade*) on the theory that their failing marriage of twenty years would weather the 1970s divorce boom better if they were to inject the sleeplessness, stress, and financial strain of a newborn child into their miserable lives. They were divorced almost immediately afterward. My mother would be married three more times: At least two of the men were functionally illiterate, and two were reliably violent. One was a former pimp who had gone into sewer work and made a pretty decent living.

You know what I learned from all that? Get the fuck out of Garbutt.

DOUGHERTY CITES THE WORK of the conservative polemicist Sam Francis, one of those old capitalism-hating conservatives who very much embraced the *paterfamilias* model of government. As in my own analysis, he finds emotional and policy links between the Trump movement and its earlier incarnation: the Pat Buchanan movement. For Dougherty, Francis provides the philosophical link. He also provides the stylistic link: He was a kook. "Francis eventually turned into a something resembling an all-out white nationalist," Dougherty writes, "penning his most racist material under a pen name. Buchanan didn't take Francis' advice in 1996, not entirely. But 20 years later, 'From Household to Nation' reads like a political manifesto from which the Trump campaign springs." It is strange to me that, even knowing this, Dougherty so hilariously misdiagnoses the conservative reaction to Trump: "A Trump win," he writes, "at least temporarily threatens the conservative movement, because it threatens to expose how inessential its ideas are to holding together the party." Dougherty also equates the fundraising engaged in by conservative organizations to the Social Security fraud that sustains his fictional Mike. Of course, there is careerism in the conservative movement—Sean Hannity *exists*—but to proceed as though it were impossible to imagine that conservatives oppose a man running (knowingly or not) on a Sam Francis platform because we oppose the loopy, crackpot, racist ideas of Sam Francis is to perform an intellectual disservice.

It is also immoral.

It is immoral because it perpetuates a lie that is destroying people's lives: that the white working class that finds itself attracted to Trump has been victimized by outside forces. It hasn't. The white working class may like the idea of Trump as a giant, pulsing, humanoid middle finger held up in the face of the Cathedral, they may sing hymns to Trump the Destroyer and whisper darkly about "globalists" and—odious, stupid term—"the Establishment," but nobody did this to them. They failed themselves.

I know, I was there, and I saw it.

Nothing happened to them. That was the great shock for me in the low life in eastern Kentucky, which isn't all that different from the low life of my native West Texas: *Nothing* happened. There wasn't some awful disaster. There wasn't a war or a famine or a plague or a foreign occupation. Even the economic changes of the past few decades do very little to explain the dysfunction and negligence—and the absolute incomprehensible *malice*—of poor white America. So, the gypsum business in Garbutt ain't what it used to be. There is more to life in the twenty-first century than wallboard and cheap sentimentality about how THE MAN closed the factories down.

Governor Reagan may have signed that original no-fault divorce law way back when, but nobody put a gun to anybody's head. The American family died because Americans killed it, and they killed it because they didn't want it. They didn't want it because they care more about themselves than they do their wives and children. *They hate their children.*

Or if they don't, you can't tell it from the way they treat them.

Dying towns? The truth about these dying communities is that they deserve to die. Economically, they are negative assets. Morally, they are indefensible. The people would be better off dispersed than forced together in self-reinforcing misery and dysfunction. Forget all that cheap theatrical Bruce Springsteen crap. Forget the sanctimony about struggling rust-belt factory towns and the conspiracies about the wily Orientals stealing our jobs. Forget your goddamned gypsum, and, if he has a problem with that, forget Ed Burke, too. The white American underclass is in thrall to a vicious, selfish culture whose main products are misery and used heroin needles. Donald Trump's rallies make them feel good. So does Fox News. So does OxyContin. What they need isn't analgesics, literal or political. They need real opportunity, which means that they need real change, which means that they need U-Haul.

If you want to live, get out of Garbutt.

I Am Cancer

Lubbock, Texas

"**M**Y CHECK DIDN'T COME."

Eviction court is not the single saddest place in the world, but if you were taking a Dantean descent through the underworld of underclass despair and dysfunction, it would be somewhere around the fourth or fifth circle. My Virgil on this journey is an actual attorney, with a suit and tie and everything, and so the judge has moved us to the end of the docket on the theory that there might be *arguments* in our case, that this litigation might turn into something resembling litigation. There are not going to be any arguments, but we get to sit through a few hours' worth of very sad stories. I think the lawyer enjoys this even less than I do, even though he gets paid, splendidly, by the hour.

The woman whose check did not come is on disability. (There's a lot of that here.) That is the check she was expecting, which did not come, for . . . some reason. Whatever her disability is, it does not appear to be the worst of her problems. She has a daughter and a man in her life (it is not clear whether he is her husband or the girl's father or both or neither), and they are obliged to maintain two separate households, "because of the domestic . . . event . . . that happened," she explains/doesn't explain.

The grammarian in me cannot help but notice that when it comes time to explain the facts of the case, the people in this courtroom rarely appear as the subjects in their own sentences. A "domestic event" just "happened," and now the man in her life cannot reside under the same roof as her daughter—or Child Protective Services will take that daughter away. Which means that after her eviction (which is never seriously in doubt) she cannot rely upon the person upon whom most people in her situation instinctively would rely.

She is not the only person whose check didn't come. The passivity and subjectlessness of these narratives is striking, and strikingly consistent. Domestic events *happen*. Checks come or don't come. (Mostly they don't.) Husbands are sent to jail because of the crime that was committed, children are taken away by the clipboard-toting minions of AUTHORITY, disease descends. The money isn't there. And, in the end, they are evicted. Bad things just happen, and, today, I am the bad thing that is just happening to one of these luckless and unhappy children of God. I am eviction, I am CPS, I am the check that didn't come. I am diabetic amputation. I am cancer.

I am, as it happens, evicting my late mother's fourth husband's fifth wife from a modest house (much more modest than the condition I left it in) in which she has resided rent-free for a decade or so. I inherited the house from my mother when she died, and her husband inherited a "life estate" in it, meaning a legal right to reside there so long as he kept current on the taxes and such. He remarried (these are marrying people) and lived there with his new wife until his life estate ended the way life estates end, and I came around to take possession of the house and sell the damned thing. They'd had years and years to prepare for this moment. Of course, they hadn't.

"Why are you doing this to us?" the woman's daughter demanded. *Because I am the bad thing that is just happening to you today, the unforeseeable event that has been hanging over you by a single hair of a horse's tail for a decade, the inevitable end of a terrible lamentation.* Getting a new place for the household might be tough—one of the people residing there, my lawyer informed me, was a registered sex offender.

These are not exactly sympathetic protagonists. But people love their sad stories. They feel compelled to tell them. Local law in Texas is pretty straightforward on the matter of evictions: If you don't pay your rent (mine is the only case today *not* involving unpaid rent), then you have to go. "Did you pay any rent in February?" the judge asks two dozen times. "Did you pay any rent in March?" The judge's power in these matters extends only to ordering (or not ordering) an eviction and ordering the payment of unpaid back rent. If a tenant wants to sue the landlord for violating the lease, or if the landlord wants to sue the tenant for failing to pay an electricity bill or damaging the property, that is a separate action. This is a yes-or-no hearing: *Did you pay the rent?* But even though the judge repeatedly explains that the sins of the landlords are irrelevant at this moment to the immediate legal question before his court, the tale must be told: *He didn't return phone calls or text messages. There were repairs left unmade. There were bedbugs.* Tenants put scarce and desperately needed money into making unlivable rental properties just barely livable. Unwritten deals were made but not honored.

"Did you pay any rent in April?"

It is different in other places that have laws making it more difficult to evict non-paying tenants. One Californian whose family owns a number of residential rental properties reports that he routinely pays deadbeats straight-up cash to vacate the premises rather than endure the trouble, expense, and uncertainty of evicting their sorry asses. I had had the same thought myself, but it quickly became clear that eviction would be the more economical route. They very much wanted to stay in the house, though not enough to offer to rent it or buy it. But certainly enough to sit tight and hope that the situation would somehow just resolve itself in their favor.

The woman I am evicting does not show up in court. (About half of those evicted decline to attend the proceedings today.) Her son attends on her behalf. My lawyer asks me five or six yes-or-no questions. The judge asks the son if he has a response. "No." He asks if he would like to present an argument. "No."

And that was that.

Of course, that's never really that. Many people who have been evicted simply refuse to leave after being ordered to, which means that they will in the end be visited by constables who remove them and their belongings from the property, often to a chorus of wailing and lamentation. And another bad thing just happens to people who, for whatever reason, have no sense of agency in their own lives.

"I'll give you a break on my rate," says my lawyer, looking at his watch. He is the son of Mexican-American farm laborers and learned at least one thing from his hard and poor childhood: Don't be a farm laborer. Law looked like a pretty good alternative, and it seems to be working out pretty well for him. The idiomatic English would be, "He became a lawyer." The better English would be, "He made himself a lawyer." How did that happen? It must have begun with decisions he made as a child or as a very young man: A leads to B leads to C leads to a good income and a nice house and a bass boat.

Writing in *National Review*, I recounted the story of Preston Smith, a man from a very poor background (think outhouses and bare feet) who walked across a wide stretch of Texas to attend college at the beginning of a career that would see him become (make himself) a successful businessman and, later, governor of Texas. He and a friend made a living in college by opening up what at the time would have been called a "filling station," a gas station–convenience store. By the time he was out of school, he had a few of them, and a movie theater, too. The reaction to that column surprised me: "That's great," critics wrote, "but he lived at a time when someone in his circumstances could open a gas station without backing and financing, and without all the taxes and regulation we have now." As though the Indian, Pakistani, and Bangladeshi immigrants who operate convenience stores from coast to coast show up in the United States with a $1 million line of business credit from Chase, an M.B.A., and a gas station waiting for them somewhere in the wilds of Oklahoma. Next time you're filling up in some lonely country location late at night, take a peek around the back of the place, and see how many of those immigrants are quietly living in the gas stations they operate. It is not uncommon, for a time. But they don't stay there long.

And while I am not much of a hard-ass on these kinds of questions (we have a positive moral obligation to help the poor, and not just the "deserving" poor), I cannot help but think of those hustling immigrants when I encounter the native-born sons and daughters of this sweet land of liberty who, if it were raining jobs and opportunity, would find a way to walk between the raindrops.

"My check didn't come."

"Did you pay any rent in January?"

"The factory closed down." "The textile jobs moved to Thailand and Vietnam." "My little town is dying." "There was an opioid addiction that happened." "My check didn't come."

"Did you pay any rent in February? In March?"

"MY CHECK DIDN'T COME."

Your check didn't come.

It's never coming.

Now what?

"Boy"

Birmingham, Alabama

"**D**OGFOOD—yeah, *dogfood*—because it looks like ground-up dog food." He's embarrassed to be talking about this. "Or sand, because it's brown. Or DIESEL. Or KILLA or 9-1-1. That's the influence of rap culture down here." He is a young, clean-cut, Eagle Scout–ish white kid, hesitant about using the words "rap culture," like he's not sure if he's allowed to say that. But he goes on, matter-of-factly. He's been off heroin for only a few months, so the details are fresh in his mind, even if he remains a little hazy on parts of his autobiographical timeline. "The 9-1-1, they call it that because they want you to know it's potent, that you'll have to go to the emergency room."

That's a weird and perverse and nasty kind of advertising, but then dope-buying psychology isn't very much like Volvo-buying psychology: Crashing is just another part of the ride. One spiteful dealer boasts about spiking his product with excessive amounts of fentanyl—a pharmaceutical analgesic used for burn victims and cancer patients—his plan being to intentionally send overdosed users to the hospital or the morgue . . . for *marketing purposes*. Once the word got out about the hideous strength of his product, that KILLA went right out the door ricky-tick.

The young man explaining the current vocabulary of opiate addiction in Birmingham is barely old enough to buy a beer, and his face and voice are soft. He describes the past several years of his life: "dope-sick and stealing," going from job to job—eight jobs in six months—robbing his employers of everything not physically nailed to the floor, alienating his family, descending. He was an addict on a mission: "You're always chasing that first shot of dope, that first high—and the first one for me almost killed me. I was seventeen or eighteen years old, and I met a guy who had just got out of prison, doing a thirteen-year sentence for heroin possession and distribution. He was staying at the Oak Mountain Lodge, which is a nice little classic place." (In 2013, four police officers and a drug dog had to be treated for exposure to dangerous chemicals after raiding a suspected meth lab in that hotel; the customer reviews online are decidedly mixed.) "I was *snorting* heroin when I met up with him, and set him up with my connect. He offered to shoot me up, and I wanted to do it. And I remember him looking me in the eyes and telling me, 'If you do this, you'll never stop, and you'll never go back.' And I said, 'Let's do it.'"

He doesn't know what happened for the next several hours. When he regained consciousness, his junkie buddy's girlfriend was worriedly ministering to him.

"That was first thing in the morning," he says. "That night, I did another one."

Same results. "I'd nodded out from snorting it, but there's nothing like shooting it."

He was, he says, a "pretty good junkie" for a time.

THIS PARTICULAR OPIATE ODYSSEY starts off in a Walgreens, something that turns out to be absolutely appropriate. I'm headed up the south coast and then inland on the heroin highway up to Atlanta, starting from the Port of Houston, which connects that city with 1,053 ports in nearly 200 countries and which in December alone welcomed the equivalent of 63,658 20-foot cargo containers of goods into the United States. There was, the feds are pretty sure, some dope squirreled away in there. In fact, all sorts of interesting stuff comes in and out of Houston. In May, U.S. Customs seized a Fast Attack Vehicle with gun mounts headed to the Netherlands. It hadn't been ordered by the Dutch military. (Organized crime in the Netherlands is bananas: A raid in the summer of 2020 found Dutch police opening up a shipping container expecting to find it loaded with narcotics or stolen goods, but what they found instead was a dentist's chair bolted to the floor and handcuffs hanging overhead—it was set up as a mobile torture chamber, God knows why.) I'm at Walgreens because I've got a long drive ahead and I'm going to be out of pocket for a bit, and I have a prescription to fill: an honest-to-goodness Schedule II Controlled Substance, in the official nomenclature, a term that covers some pretty interesting stuff, including the oxycodone and fentanyl I'll be hearing so much about in the next few days. Some of us are going to heaven, some of us are going to hell, but all of us have to stop at Walgreens first.

The clerk is on the phone with a doctor's office: "What's your DEA number?"

FOR WORKING-CLASS WHITE GUYS WHO HAVEN'T FOUND THEIR WAY INTO THE GOOD JOBS in the energy economy or the related manufacturing and construction booms that have reverberated throughout the oil patch, who aren't college-bound or in possession of the skills to pay the bills, things aren't looking so great: While much of the rest of the world gets healthier and longer-lived, the average life expectancy for white American men without college educations is declining. Angus Deaton, the Princeton economist who won the Nobel Prize in 2015, ran the numbers and found (in a study co-authored by his Princeton colleague Anne Case) that what's killing what used to be the white working class isn't diabetes or heart disease or the consumption of fatty foods and Big Gulps that so terrifies Michael Bloomberg, but alcohol-induced liver failure, along with overdoses of opioid prescription painkillers and heroin: Wild Turkey and hillbilly heroin, and regular old heroin, too, the use of which has increased dramatically in recent years as medical and law-enforcement authorities crack down on the wanton overprescription of oxy and related painkillers.

Which is to say: While we were *ignoring* criminally negligent painkiller prescriptions, we helped create a gigantic population of opioid addicts, and then, when we started paying attention, the first thing we did was take away the legal (and quasi-legal) stuff produced to exacting clinical standards by Purdue Pharma (maker of OxyContin) and others. So: lots of opiate addicts, fewer prescription opiates.

What was left was DIESEL, SAND—*dogfood*.

The clerks at this Walgreens are super friendly, but the place is set up security-wise like a bank, and that's to be expected. This particular location was knocked over by a young white man with a gun the summer before last, an addict who had been seen earlier lurking around the CVS down the road. This is how you know you're a pretty good junkie: The robber walked in and pointed his automatic at the clerk and demanded oxy first, then a bottle of Tusinex cough syrup, and then, almost as an afterthought, the $90 in the till. Walgreens gets robbed a lot: In January, armed men stormed the Walgreens in Edina, Minnesota, and stole $8,000 worth of drugs, mainly oxy. In October, a sneaky young white kid in an Iowa State sweatshirt made off with more than $100,000 worth of drugs—again, mainly oxy and related opioid painkillers, from a Walgreens in St. Petersburg, Florida. Other Walgreens locations—in Liberty, Kansas; East Bradford, Pennsylvania; Elk Grove, California; Kaysville, Utah; Virginia Beach; New Orleans—all have been hit by armed robbers or sneak thieves over the past year or so, and there have been many more oxy thefts.

It won't make the terrified clerks feel any better, but there's poetic justice in that: In 2013, Walgreens paid the second-largest fine ever imposed under the Controlled Substances Act for being so loosey-goosey in handling oxy at its distribution center in Jupiter, Florida, that it enabled untold quantities of the stuff to reach the black market. The typical pharmacy sells 73,000 oxycodone pills a year; six Walgreens in

Florida were going through more than 1 million pills a year—each. A few years before that, Purdue was fined $634.5 million for misleading the public about the addictiveness of oxycodone. Kentucky, which has been absolutely ravaged by opiate addiction, is still pursuing litigation against Purdue, and it has threatened to take its case all the way to the Supreme Court, if it comes to that.

Ground Zero in the opiate epidemic isn't some exotic Taliban-managed poppy field or some cartel boss's fortified compound: It's right there at Walgreens, in the middle of every city and town in the country.

I pick up my prescription and get on my way.

The next afternoon, having driven past billboards advertising boudin and strip joints with early-bird lunch specials and casino after casino after sad little casino; help-wanted signs for drilling-fluid businesses and the Tiger Truck Stop (which has a twenty-four-hour Cajun café and an actual no-kidding *live tiger* in a cage out front); past Whiskey Bay and Contraband Bayou, where the pirate Jean Lafitte once stashed his booty; around the Port of New Orleans, another *entrepôt* for heroin and cocaine—it is almost as close to Cartagena as it is to New York—I arrive at a reasonably infamous New Orleans drug corner, where I inquire as discreetly as I can about the availability of prescription painkillers, which are getting harder and harder to find on the street.

Until recently, this particular area was under the control of an energetic fellow called "Dumplin," who, judging from his police photos, isn't nearly so cute and approachable as that nickname would suggest. Dumplin ran a gang called 3NG, which presumably stands for "Third and Galvez," the nearby intersection that constituted the center of his business empire.[1] In March, Dumplin went away on three manslaughter charges and a raft of drug-conspiracy complaints. The opiate trade doesn't seem to have noticed. Little teams of two or three loiter in residential doorways, and business gets done. Who is running the show now? Somebody knows.

Everybody has heroin, but my inquiry about oxy is greeted as a breach of protocol by my not especially friendly neighborhood drug dealer, who doesn't strike me as the kind of guy who suffers breaches of protocol lightly. He looks at me with exactly the sort of contempt one would expect from a captain of an industry that uses lethal overdoses as a marketing gimmick.

"This ain't *Walgreens*, motherfucker."

"WE PARTNER WITH WALGREENS." If Dr. Peter DeBlieux sometimes sounds as if he's seen it all, it's possible that he has. As his name suggests, he's a New Orleans local, and he has been practicing medicine in the city long enough to have seen earlier heroin epidemics. Now the chief medical officer and medical-staff president at University Medical Center, he speaks with some authority on how changes in global heroin logistics affect conditions in his emergency rooms, which have just seen a 250 percent spike in opiate-overdose cases in one month.

"The first time we'd seen these numbers is when the heroin supply chain moved from the Orient to South America. Before that, New Orleans's supply traditionally came with everybody else's supply, from the Far East through New York, and then down to us. By the time it got to New Orleans, it was adulterated, much less pure. But then competitors from South America began bringing heroin along the same routes used to import cocaine. They brought a purer product, which meant more overdoses requiring rescue." That was in the late 1980s and early 1990s, right around the time when our self-appointed media scolds were bewailing the "heroin chic" in Calvin Klein fashion shoots and celebrity junkie Kurt Cobain was nodding off during publicity events.

The current spike in overdoses is related to a couple of things. One proximate cause is the increased use of fentanyl to spike heroin. Heroin, like Johnnie Walker, is a blend: The raw stuff is cut with fillers to increase the volume, and then that diluted product is spiked with other drugs to mask the effects of dilution. Enter the fentanyl. Somebody, somewhere, has got his hands on a large supply of the stuff, either hijacked from legitimate pharmaceutical manufacturers or produced in some narco black site in Latin America or China for the express purpose of turbocharging heroin. (Where did it come from? Somebody knows.) Fentanyl, on its own, isn't worth very much on the street: It might get you numb, but it really doesn't get you high, and such pleasures as are to be derived from its recreational use are powerfully offset by its tendency to kill you dead. But if the blend is artfully done, then fentanyl can make stepped-on heroin feel more potent than it is. If the blend isn't right . . . medical personnel are known to refer to that as a "clean kill."

New Orleans has taken some steps to try to get ahead of this mess. One of the things that the city's health providers had been experimenting with was giving addicts and their families prescriptions for naloxone, sold under the brand name Narcan, which is the anti-intoxicant used to reverse the effects of opiates in people who have overdosed. Put another way: The best clinical thinking at the moment—the top idea among our best and brightest white-coated elite—is *to help junkies pre-plan their overdoses*. If that's shocking and depressing, what's more shocking and depressing is that it really is needful. Essential, even. A few other cities have experimented with it, too, and not long after my conversation with Dr. DeBlieux, New Orleans's top health officials handed down an emergency order to make Narcan available over the counter. Jeffrey Elder, the city's director of emergency medical services, said that with the New Orleans emergency rooms seeing as many as ten opiate overdoses a day, the step was necessary. Dr. DeBlieux's emergency rooms saw seven overdose deaths in January alone.

There are stirrings of awareness in high places about heroin's most recent ferocious comeback, but it has taken a while. Congress held hearings, and Senator Kelly Ayotte, the charismatic young New Hampshire Republican, introduced the Heroin and Prescription Opioid Abuse Prevention, Education, and Enforcement Act of 2015, currently on ice in the Judiciary Committee. That bill would . . . convene a task force.

Dr. DeBlieux compares the public perception of heroin to the public perception of AIDS (the issues are not entirely unrelated) a generation ago: It is seen as a problem for deviants. AIDS was for perverts who liked to have anonymous sex with men at highway rest stops, and heroin is a problem for toothless pillbillies who turn to the needle after running out of oxy and for whores and convicts and menacing black men in New Orleans ghettos. Heroin, this line of thinking goes, is a problem for people who deserve it.

"Nobody cares, because of who is affected," Dr. DeBlieux says—or who is perceived to be affected. "There are two problems with that. One, it's unethical. Two, it isn't true." It isn't just the born-to-lose crowd and career criminals and deviants and undesirables. It's working-class white men and college-bound suburban kids, too.

Dr. DeBlieux and his colleagues are doing what they can to minimize the damage. University Medical Center distributes that Narcan through a private embedded pharmacy in the hospital, operated by—you won't be surprised—Walgreens.

ODYSSEY HOUSE IS NOT A HAPPY PLACE. It's a necessary place.

I arrive too early for my appointment, so I have a look around the neighborhood. It is downscale, and there definitely is a little bit of unlicensed pharmaceutical trade being transacted nearby, but it's far from the worst I've seen in New Orleans. I decide to go pick up some extra notebooks, and I end up—inevitably—at Walgreens. There are 8,173 Walgreens locations filling 894 million prescriptions a year, and that big ol' record-book fine doesn't look big up against $77 billion in sales a year. CVS does $140 billion a year, filling one-third of all U.S. pharmaceutical prescriptions. In a country of 319 million, there were 259 million opiate-painkiller prescriptions written last year. There were 47,000 lethal overdoses in the U.S. in 2014, almost 30,000 of which were prescription painkillers and heroin. Some 94 percent of heroin users told researchers that they got into heroin because the pills they started on became too expensive or too difficult to find, whereas heroin is cheap and plentiful. How do we keep up with all those pills? Where do they go? Somebody knows. It's been only two weeks since there was an armed robbery of a Walgreens in New Orleans, but it wasn't this one. That one is about 20 minutes away.

I park my car on the street across from Odyssey House, down the block from a sign advertising free HIV screening, and an older white man comes out of his home to stand on the porch, staring at me. He's still there, still staring, when I go inside the building across the street.

Odyssey House is the largest addiction-treatment facility in Louisiana, treating about seven hundred people a month, about half of them from greater New Orleans. It was founded in response to New Orleans's first major heroin epidemic, some forty-five years ago. Its clients are predominantly male, and about half of them are white in a city that isn't. About 50 percent of its clients are there on court orders; the other half have simply decided that they want to live. Its CEO, Ed Carlson, has a master's in clinical psychology and not many kind words for Louisiana's former governor, conservative health-policy wonk Bobby Jindal. It's partly a familiar complaint—Jindal's rejection of the Medicaid expansion under the Affordable Care Act means that about 90 percent of Odyssey House's patients have to be covered by general state funds, which are scarce. But it's also an illustration of one of the hidden costs of privatizing public-health services: the transfer of administrative costs from state agencies onto third parties, including nonprofits such as Odyssey House.

"Under the privatization of the Bayou Health plans," Carlson says, "it's like this: I have a guy who shows up, who's a heroin addict, who's been in and out of the criminal justice system, maybe a twenty-year heroin addict, maybe semi-homeless, and he wants to get off heroin in our detox. And I have to spend an hour explaining to [insurance bureaucrats] why this guy needs treatment, usually with someone who doesn't understand treatment at all." That meant hiring more administrative help. "What it did was, it shot up our costs. Now we have people who all they do all day long is sit down and try to convince somebody that this person needs treatment. And they'll say, 'Has he tried outpatient?' He's a heroin addict. He's homeless. He's here at our door. I don't have a problem justifying to them that a person needs services, but, once we've justified it, then let's go with the level of services that a medical professional recommends."

Outpatient treatment? Heroin addicts as a class don't have a real good record for keeping appointments.

Odyssey's program is intensive: It begins with a medically supported detox program, which isn't all that critical for opiate addicts (the popular image of the effects of heroin withdrawal are theatrically exaggerated, as Theodore Dalrymple documented in his classic on the subject, *Romancing Opiates*) but which is absolutely necessary for alcohol withdrawal, which can be fatal. And the reality is that most heroin addicts drink their fair share, too. Detox is followed by a twenty-eight-day residential program, followed by housing support and an outpatient program. Odyssey has primary-care physicians and psychiatrists on staff, a separate residential program for adolescents, and more. They aren't promiscuous with the money—for example, they don't send methamphetamine addicts to detox, because their withdrawal lasts only a few hours and its main effects are discomfort and a few days of insomnia—but, even so, all this treatment gets expensive, and the city of New Orleans kicks in the princely sum of $0.00 in municipal money for these services, with the exception of some pass-through money from state and federal agencies.

The medical consensus is that this sort of treatment provides the best chance for helping *some*—fewer than you'd think—of the chronically addicted, homeless and semi-homeless, destitute, low-bottom population. There's no cheap way to do it. "There's really only two things we know, from a scientific standpoint, about addiction," Carlson says. "The first thing we know is that when a person has a problem with addiction and they have that moment, that break in the wall of denial—if they can access treatment at that point, then they're more likely to engage in the treatment process and to be more serious about it. The other thing we know is that the longer we keep people in treatment, the longer they're going to stay clean and sober."

In total, it costs just under $1 million a month to run Odyssey House and provide those services to its seven hundred or so patients. And what do the funding agencies get for that money? A one-year success rate of a little more than 50 percent—which is significantly better than that of most comparable programs. Beyond that one year? No one really knows. "The fact is that most people who need addiction treatment don't really want it," Carlson says.

It isn't clear that there really is a solution to the opiate epidemic, but if there is, there's one thing you can be sure of: It is going to cost a great deal of money. "We have waiting lists for all our programs," Carlson says with a slight grimace. "We could probably double in size and still have waiting lists."

HOMELESSNESS IN NEW ORLEANS isn't the only model of heroin addiction, or even the most prevalent one. Up in the land of Whole Foods and Starbucks and yoga studios in one of the nicer parts of Birmingham, it looks like a different world. But it isn't. More white people, more Volvos—same junkies.

Danny Malloy doesn't sound like he belongs here. He has a heavy Boston accent, and he still shakes his head at some aspects of life in the South: "We measure snow in feet up there, but it's inches down here," he scoffs. There's a little snow blowing around, and a few streaks of white on the grass. "No plows, no salt trucks, and nobody knows how to drive in it." He ended up in Alabama the way people end up places. His parents were divorced when he was very young, his alcoholic father eventually sent him to live with an aunt, and he later sought out his estranged mother in Birmingham. "I didn't know her," he says. He was already a blackout drunk and had found his way to the pills, which he was both consuming and dealing.

"I never realized I had a problem. I thought I was having a good time. I got into prescription pills. I really liked them—I mean like *really* liked them. It took probably three years of me dabbling in those before I was fully addicted, and every day I had to have Lortabs. I got into OxyContin and was selling those. I got set up by someone and sold to an undercover police officer. So I was arrested for distribution, and I was facing time. At that point, someone came along and said, 'These pills are expensive, and you can't sell them anymore. So why don't you do heroin?' I said I would never do that. I don't want to use a needle. But, eventually, like a good drug addict, I was like, 'Let me try that.' The rest was history. I've been to fifteen or twenty rehabs, including psychiatric hospitals, arrests, detoxes, methadone rehabs. I couldn't get rid of it. I did that for about seven years. Things got . . . really bad." He'd been a college student, majoring in "whatever started at noon," but he ended up being kicked out. "The first time I ever thought maybe I had a problem was when I got arrested and my face was down in a puddle with a cop on my back. That's what it took." Eventually, he put himself on a Greyhound and checked into the Foundry, a Christian rehab facility. "I never looked back. I turned my life over to God, and he took away the desire to use." He pauses as if reconsidering what he's said. "It isn't magic."

Alabama doctors write more opiate prescriptions per capita than those of any other state. And where there is oxy, there will be dogfood. "The pills lead to heroin," Malloy says. "You see these doctors getting arrested for running a pill mill. Well, they have hundreds of people they're prescribing to, and when they tighten down on that, the next thing is the heroin."

Far from being an inner-city problem and a poor white problem, heroin is if anything more prevalent in some of the wealthier areas around Birmingham, says Drew Callner, another recovering addict and a volunteer at the Addiction Prevention Coalition in Birmingham, a faith-based organization aimed at realistic preventative measures and connecting addicts with recovery resources. "Heroin is easier to get, and it's cheaper." Callner's father was a child psychologist, he was planning on becoming one himself, and he was a trust-funder—twice. "Yeah, I blew through two trusts," he says, snorting.

He'd been a Marine and wanted to become a firefighter, but the only thing he could commit to for the long term—fifteen years—was oxy and heroin. Beyond the depleted trust funds, the deficit that seems to weigh on him most heavily is that of time. He is thirty-two years old and has spent nearly half of his life as an active drug user. "Going back to school is interesting," he says. "I'm in some English 101 class at 8:30 in the morning, that I've taken four or five times"—there were five or six colleges, and five rehabs in four years—"and I'm in there with a bunch of eighteen- and nineteen-year-olds. It's humbling. Humiliating. But when you get sober, you need something to ground you."

He'd derailed his life before it had really gotten underway, but his roommates in his last residential program—which he got out of just last week, with seven months' sobriety—were a personal-injury attorney, a senior banker, and an accountant.

"And then there was me. "

THEY CALL IT THE "RED FLAG." Some heroin addicts fall in love with the ritual of shooting up. Some of them have been known to shoot up when they don't have any heroin, just to feel the calming presence of the needle in the arm. The ritual is familiar enough to anybody who has spent any time in that world: You put the chunk of tar or bit of powder in the spoon, squirt a little water in with the syringe, heat it up to get it to dissolve, drop a little pinch of cotton into the spoon for a filter, pull the heroin solution up through the cotton into the syringe, find a vein—this isn't always easy, and it gets harder—work the needle in, pull the plunger back . . .

And then, you see it: the RED FLAG, a little flash of blood that gets pulled into the syringe and lets you know that you have found a vein, that you aren't about to waste your junk on an intramuscular injection that isn't going to do anything except burn and waste your money and disappoint you and leave you with a heroin blister. Certain addicts become, for whatever reason, almost as addicted to the needle—and addicted to the RED FLAG, to the sight of their own blood being extracted—as to the heroin itself.

"When I couldn't get heroin, I would just shoot anything," Malloy says. "I would load up hot water and shoot it, just to feel the needle. I had to load it up and shoot it—it was a routine. So I started shooting Xanax, Klonopin, trying to shoot Vicodin, but that never works."

"I was the opposite," Callner says. "Every time I shot up, I would hear my mom's voice, telling me I'm a piece of shit. Plus, I'm not very vascular, so I had to shoot up on the outside of my arm, which meant looking at myself in the mirror. There was just something about that, five or six times a day, looking yourself in the eye and seeing the deterioration. And hating it."

"I remember using dull, dull needles, and having to stab myself until I found a vein," recovering addict Dalton Smith says. "But I was obsessed with when you got the needle in, and pulling it back and seeing the blood. The RED FLAG." Smith sometimes shot up imaginary heroin, convinced that bits of carpet lint were heroin. "The fuzz—I remember seeing the fuzz from the carpet in my rig."

None of these guys comes from Heartbreak Hill. Some of them came from some money, came from good schools, went to college, had successful, high-income parents. But there was also divorce and addiction in the family—one young recovering addict is in the precarious situation of having to live with his alcoholic father—and a general sense of directionlessness. They are from that great vast America whose people simultaneously have too much and too little.

One or two breaks in a different direction, and Dalton Smith might have been the youth minister at your church. (He still might be.) He's got that heartbreakingly distinctive shamefacedness that you see whenever you're around young addicts or young prisoners (there's some substantial overlap on that Venn diagram) or other young people with woeful self-inflicted injuries, a shadow across the face that says that while he may be trying to have faith in whatever Higher Power that sets His almighty hand on recovering junkies in Alabama, that everything happens for a reason, and that he's right where he's supposed to be, he'd really give anything to be able to go back and change one thing on that chain of decisions that led to his messing his life up nearly irreparably before he was old enough to rent a car from Avis. He's twenty-two years old. There's a long chain of bad decisions that goes back to the beginning of his self-destructive career as a drug addict, and at its beginning is a twelve-year-old child. Ten years later, he knows a lot of words for heroin.

"Down here, they sometimes call it 'BOY.'"

The Weed Man Is All Up in the Chamber of Commerce

Denver

THE WEED MAN HAS EMERGED FROM THE SHADOWS. He has come out from the seedy backrooms and dank basement apartments, and he is all up in the Chamber of Commerce. The Weed Man has acquired himself a suit, a tie, and a marketing department. Drive down I-70 in Denver and you'll see those Good Samaritan highway-beautification signs sponsored by Metro Cannabis, along with signs for Green Solutions, "Colorado's #1 Marijuana Dispensary!" and Grow Big Supply, a purveyor of hydroponic agricultural goods, which is advertising an "industry mixer," a good old-fashioned, vendor-networking, business-card-swapping event for major-league pro potheads, an event, culturally speaking, one step removed from a Rotary luncheon, even if the evening does have the astrologically inevitable Bob Marley theme: "Grow Big Supply is proud to present Reggae Night, the first Thursday of every month from 6 to 10 p.m. Each month we serve different hand-crafted cocktails, a variety of foods, live music, and, of course, the Grow Big Go-Go girls." The Weed Man may not have much of an imagination, but your local Masonic temple or Elks lodge probably doesn't have a squadron of go-go girls, which is why freemasonry and Elkery are moribund but the future of marijuana, weed, hash, Kush, kind, sticky, nugs,

cheeba, Cambodian red, fluffy yellow hydroponic blossoms from parts
unknown, edibles, Dixie Elixirs Premium Marijuana-Infused Products,
cannabis-extraction machines with the heat provided by CO_2 instead of
butane because we're all a bit concerned about neural hypoxia, THC-
bearing chocolates and caramels and Keef Kat bars and Rasta Reese's
ganja-packed peanut-butter cups, terrifyingly clinical-looking syringes
for the sublingual delivery of concentrated cannabis extract, cannabutter
and Taboo Confections Lemon Shortbread Tarts ("KEEP OUT OF REACH
OF CHILDREN"), Baked-brand confections, and a hundred thousand
resplendently sumptuous variations on the theme of $C_{12}H_{22}O_{11}+$
$C_{21}H_{30}O_2$ is bright, bright, bright indeed.

Come, come shelter under the sign of the glowing green cross.

In 2000, Colorado legalized the possession of marijuana for medical purposes through Amendment 20, a constitutional referendum. It
permitted possession of up to two ounces of marijuana or up to six
marijuana plants on the condition that at least three of them be seedlings
not yet producing usable weed. There was some tussling over how many
patients a caregiver could provide with marijuana—that is, over when
somebody stops being a *caregiver* and starts being a drug dealer—and
in 2010 the state enacted C.R.S. 12-43.3-101 *et seq.*, the Colorado Medical Marijuana Code. Medical marijuana was legal, and it was good. But
it was also kind of a load of bunk—sure, marijuana has some therapeutic
qualities, but the main attractive quality of marijuana is that it gets you
high as a Georgia pine and makes *Super Troopers* really, really funny.
In November 2012, Colorado voters decided to take things one step
further than medical-marijuana states such as California had—which is
to say, they decided to stop pretending and go ahead and end marijuana
prohibition per se, legalizing its recreational consumption and establishing an expanded regulatory apparatus, the Marijuana Enforcement
Division, to oversee commercial activity related to that consumption.
The stoners in Colorado rejoiced.

The cops in Nebraska? Not so much.

Get a little ways out of Denver's self-consciously hipsterish "we were Austin before people remembered they hated freezing their asses off" zone of gluten-free urbanity and you are right back in weird old savage prairie America, endless acres of buffalo grass and purple-flowering skunk weed (not that kind of skunk weed! *Polemonium viscosum*) with Colorado's vast, empty spaces leading to Nebraska and its collection of vaster, emptier spaces, the sort of geography that makes you constantly aware of how much gas you have in the tank. It is the end of May, and the rest of the country is gearing up for Memorial Day weekend, the informal opening days of summer. In Deuel County, Nebraska, just over the line from Colorado, they're having a snowstorm.

This has been smuggling country since forever, basically. In the late 1800s, the brutal gunman and dandy Luke Short set up shop in nearby Sidney and made his fortune selling whiskey to the Sioux in violation of federal law, shooting customers who became troublesome. In the Deuel County seat, Chappell ("The Extra 'L' Is for 'Living the Good Life,'" according to the billboard at the edge of town), Sheriff Adam Hayward is dealing with a less colorful sort of outlaw: sundry Midwestern marijuana aficionados who traverse his state to and from (and it is from that is mostly the problem) the legal-weed promised land of Colorado, bringing sticky green contraband to Nebraska but also to Illinois, Indiana, Minnesota, and places beyond. He estimates that about every fifth traffic stop now results in the discovery of something that should not be there, and he has had to lock up many more people than he ever has in the past.

"Nebraska doesn't *have* to arrest them," one critic says. That's true at some level, of course. But the reality is that Nebraska has pretty liberal marijuana laws, and you kind of have to be a jerk to get locked up: A first-possession offense with less than an ounce is basically a parking ticket ($300, no possibility of jail time), and you have to be on your third offense before you can see even a week in jail—and seven days, plus a fine of up to $500, is the maximum sentence. You have to be packing more than a pound of weed through the Cornhusker State before you've committed a felony. So, no, Sheriff Hayward doesn't have to arrest you for an ounce of marijuana—but 110 pounds?

Yeah, at that point he kind of has to arrest you.

Sheriff Hayward is a local, a youngish and no-nonsense man whose office is wallpapered with certificates from the likes of the Mid-States Organized Crime Information Center and the Nebraska Law Enforcement Intelligence Network. He is not an admirer of Colorado's legalization effort: His office is a big piece of the budget in this county of fewer than two thousand, and his incarceration expenses have quadrupled since Colorado's marijuana dispensaries opened their doors to the public. This in a place that had been so quiet that there is no county jail—Deuel County contracts out its jailing to nearby communities. Out of a $290,000 sheriff's-department budget, some $140,000 goes to incarceration expenses, and the county's tax revenue has been strained by the burden.

"The interstate brings a lot of trouble," the sheriff says. "Sometimes, I wish it wasn't there."

That trouble does not generally take the form of people driving over the state line with the amount of marijuana that can be sold to them legally in Colorado. Nonresidents are welcome to shop in Colorado's dispensaries, but they are prohibited from buying more than seven grams in a single transaction, and transactions are monitored in order to prevent bulk purchases' being disguised as tiny transactions. You would have to make more than six thousand legal purchases from one of Colorado's dispensaries to put together one of those hundred-pound packages the Nebraska authorities are taking out of cars. In spite of the regulations, those purchases do get made, though probably not from the dispensary operators; Sheriff Hayward theorizes that marijuana is diverted from a few steps up the production chain, at the grow houses. The Drug Enforcement Administration has even claimed (apply DEA-credibility discount here) that, far from knocking the Mexican drug cartels out of the marijuana business, high-quality U.S.-grown weed is so profitable that the syndicates are trafficking smoke from the United States into Mexico rather than the other way around. In 2014, a series of federal raids in

Colorado were conducted as part of an investigation linking the state's legal operations to Colombian drug cartels.

But if the jail records in Sheriff Hayward's office are any indication, you don't have to be Pablo Escobar to make a killing exploiting the interstate inconsistencies in marijuana prohibition. Not long ago, his department arrested four young men from Minnesota, ages sixteen and seventeen, who were pulled over driving eighty-six miles per hour in a seventy-five-mile-per-hour zone on a Sunday afternoon and discovered with a pound or so of marijuana. It turned out that this was a regular thing for them. "They were coming down every week and buying $2,500 to $3,000 worth of marijuana, which they could sell for $6,000 back home," Hayward says. He pauses. "That's more money than I make. A lot more."

He mentions that there is a dispensary about twenty minutes away in Sedgwick, Colorado. He is not the only person to single out that establishment: Sedgwick has a population of fewer than two hundred people, but it is home to a marijuana dispensary as large and well stocked as those you'll find in Denver. In weed as in real estate: location, location, location.

FUNNY THING about Sedgwick Alternative Relief (motto: "THE FIRST DISPENSARY IN COLORADO," which is a geographical rather than temporal claim), the marijuana retailer nearest the Nebraska border: Among the cars parked out front, there is not a single one with Colorado plates. There are cars from Nebraska, Illinois, Indiana, and so forth, but not one from the state in which the establishment is actually located. There are some Colorado plates in front of the gardening-supply store next door, which, like the dispensary, is marked with the great glowing green cross sign that has become the universal symbol of legal retail marijuana. It is a little discombobulating: Sure, you expect to see a bar nearby with a sign reading "Coors on Tap" and the Sedgwick Antique Inn, because marijuana tourism is a thing. But to be assaulted by the overwhelming vegetal smell of all that high-grade doobage, the Mahatma-brand concentrate products and the "recycler bubble oil rigs" (whatever the *hell* those are), and to take in the "awesome, dude" vibe of it all within sight of lowing, dusty cattle and bales of hay—it's just weird.

The clientele at Sedgwick Alternative Relief during my visit was almost uniformly old—not even plausibly middle-aged, but gray and creaky and not looking exactly what you'd call *hale* or *prosperous*. But that's pretty common in remote small-town farming America, pop-culture romanticism notwithstanding, and it's hard to disaggregate the effects of lifelong stonerdom from those of simply living the low version of country life. The clients come out of the shop with their brown paper bags of product, get into their cars, and drive toward whatever state boundary it is that they're probably not supposed to be crossing.

Inside, there's a waiting room with a few unhappy-looking old people in it and a security partition separating the general stoner public from the green gold beyond. A cute and chipper young woman who speaks in the pothead patois that one encounters everywhere in Weed World and that seems to be at least as much a product of culture as of chemistry greets me warmly and instantly cools a degree (or seven) when I tell her I am a reporter and ask whether I can speak to the owner. She does that Japanese-style thing where she makes it clear that that is not going to happen without actually saying "That is not going to happen." In a display of pro forma cooperativeness, she takes my number.

"Did you want to buy some product while you're here?" The price is seventeen dollars a gram. I haven't had marijuana in a long time that is nonetheless not as long a time as it really should be for a man my age, and the thought of smoking a joint is vaguely repugnant. But the tinctures? The chocolates? The THC lollipops? Television is not all you might hope it would be in the motels of rural Nebraska, and I didn't sleep well last night, and there's a moment of . . . but, no.

"Okay! Well, thanks for coming in!"

The thing about the marijuana business: It's business.

"THERE'S THAT ONE IN, UH, THAT'S RIGHT THERE AT NEBRASKA, that everybody's mad at?" Sasha Saghbazarian, a "bud-tender" (which is what they call a salesman) at Pure Medical Dispensary in Denver, is very helpful and a great deal more put together than you might think on first impression, given that she has the spacey affect that is apparently universal in her profession. I ask her whether she means the one in Sedgwick, and she communicates the affirmative.

Pure Medical has an absolutely spectacular showroom, one part mad scientist's lair (my bud-tender is very excited to show me the butane-free carbon dioxide–based thingamabob that they use to extract marijuana essence from the plant itself, which apparently is the best-practices way of doing it) and one part high-end boulangerie, spotless display cases packed with many varieties of old-fashioned smokable marijuana—which turns out to be sort of passé as the offerings go—and a whole lot more in the way of edibles (store brand name: "Incr-edibles") and concentrates (the dabs and wax and so forth that the old-fashioned gray-bearded weed hounds warn will *mess you up, boy*) and an assortment of capsules: "The black one is for nighttime," Sasha says. "It's a sleep aid. The white one is for during the day. The red one is for pain. The green one is an aphrodisiac, for all that fun stuff." She giggles. *Sleep aid?* I think about the flight home. And then I think about dealing with TSA while high on CO_2-extracted THC, and tell myself that I am really too old to be thinking about this, but, still, there's a moment of . . . but, no.

For those who aren't feeling too old, there's a bunch of candy, which turns out to be sort of problematic from a regulatory point of view. Sasha is better versed on the rules than almost anybody I talk to, and one of the things she points out is that the Gummi Bear doppelgängers are on their way out: THE MAN has decided that weed candy that is designed to look like familiar brands of conventional candy (much of it festooned with similar labels and given porn-star-style pun names—BuddahFinger bars, for example) is a danger to the little ones and shall henceforth be banned. But as Sasha points out, the non-copycat candies can be a problem for adults, who sometimes eat the candy like it is candy and get themselves waaaaaaaaaay tooooooooooo high, which can be a very uncomfortable experience. Rather than taking the sensible ten-milligram dose and then waiting for a couple of hours to see whether they really want more, she says, consumers sometimes just wolf down waaaaaaaaaay toooooooooo muuuuch.

So that's one thing. But there is a whole lot more on the regulatory front. Not a Colorado resident? Can't work in a dispensary. Got convictions? Can't work in a dispensary. Got unpaid child support? Can't work in a dispensary. Got bad credit? If your financial situation is bad enough that THE MAN thinks that you might be tempted to, say, cut a side deal with some shady Colombians, you can't work in a dispensary. Sasha talks about the "secret shopper" agents dispatched by the Marijuana Enforcement Division, who visit dispensaries unannounced and try to trick the bud-tenders into breaking one of the myriad regulations under which they conduct their blissed-out business. They will talk about transporting marijuana across state lines, at which point bud-tenders are expected to give them a stern-faced warning that this is a state and federal no-no.

There are rules to the high life, damn it.

THERE IS, IN FACT, A WHOLE COMPLICATED TECHNO-LOGISTICAL machine at work keeping track of every bud and brownie: Shipments of marijuana products are RFID-tagged, sales are tracked by weight (in the case of actual marijuana) or units (in the case of capsules, pills, edibles, and so forth), and a government database (sorry to harsh your buzz with that terrifying phrase, dude) called "METRC"—pronounced "metric," the Marijuana Enforcement, Tracking, Reporting, and Compliance system—developed by the supply-chain and logistics-technology company Franwell, keeps track of every legal transaction in something close to real time. Sasha utters the name "METRC" with heavy respect; John Hudak of the Brookings Institution calls it "the backbone of Colorado's regulatory structure governing legalized marijuana." Nothing's perfect, of course. "There will always be a few nugs that fall on the floor," Sasha says. "They're looking for bulk."

So how do people end up in Sheriff Hayward's jurisdiction with pounds and pounds of Colorado weed that they are not supposed to have? "They know how to cheat the system, to grow extra," the sheriff says. "In a way, it's ten times worse than it was. The problem used to be one guy with 100 pounds of marijuana. Now it's 100 guys with one pound of marijuana." And what does he think about Colorado's vast regulatory structure? "Nobody's following the rules over there."

Regulation is hard work. As Sheriff Hayward points out, his state has 247 different laws to enforce when it comes to alcohol. "In Prohibition, there was just one law: It's illegal." And that is how he'd prefer to see marijuana treated. And so would the powers that be in his state, along with their counterparts in Oklahoma, who are suing Colorado on the grounds that its marijuana laws are unconstitutional (the theory being that those laws are a state attempt to preempt federal drug laws) and that Colorado's liberalization has imposed heavy costs on other states. Beyond the instinctive "mind your own damned business" defense, Colorado points to its colonoscopic regulatory machinery as evidence of its good faith and political responsibility. But if there is one thing that is predictable in matters regulatory, it is that the regulators will concentrate their efforts on the parties that are easiest to regulate, which in this case are the dispensaries and their gaggles of earnest bud-tenders, who seem very, very happy to be *marijuana professionals*. Cartel infiltrators up the supply chain? That's a different matter. The dispensary operators have an incentive to keep a lid on criminal hijinks for the same reason that big corporate strip-club operators work diligently to keep prostitution out of their businesses and that Las Vegas is the American city in which you will be most rigorously prosecuted for organizing an illegal poker game: The legit business pays so well that crime holds little attraction for them—in fact, it represents unwanted competition.

THE COLORADO MARIJUANA BUSINESS is in its 1963 Las Vegas–casino period: The vice itself has been legalized, the Chamber of Commerce is deploying in force, and the organized-crime tough guys are about to find out what ruthlessness, iron will, and intense singularity of purpose really mean as the publicly traded multinational corporations take over their rackets and hand them their heads. You think you're a gangster? Try picking a fight with Walt Disney. It isn't pretty, but in the end you'd rather be dealing with the Marijuana Enforcement Division and some mutant variation of Monsanto or Johnson & Johnson than with the wild boys from Culiacán or Beltrán-Leyva Inc.

That is the economic theory behind marijuana legalization. But how to resolve the realities, which are that Colorado wants legal weed while Nebraska and Oklahoma do not, and that the presence of black markets in prohibition states ensures the presence of black markets and gray markets in legalization states? The prohibition states are asking for federal action, but if there is anything we've learned from our endless and endlessly stupid war on drugs, it is that federal action generally makes things worse. One can sympathize with the desire of people in the prohibition states to keep drugs out of their communities, but it is more difficult to sympathize with their desire to avoid paying the freight for their decisions—especially when their prohibition imposes costs on legalization states just as legalization in those states imposes costs on them. Weed-whacking is an expensive business.

In the long run, legal marijuana will probably go the way that legal gambling and prostitution have: less crime, more responsible business practices, and the slow, gentle normalization of what once was verboten. The Weed Man of old is fading—long live the Chamber of Commerce.

The Wisenheimers of Cabrini-Green

Chicago

"**H**EY, MAN. HEY, MAN. WHAT YOU NEED?" The question is part solicitation, part challenge, and the challenge part is worth paying attention to in a city with more than five hundred murders a year. The question comes from a young, light-skinned black guy with freckles. We're in the shadow of what used to be the infamous Cabrini-Green housing projects, only a fifteen-minute walk from the Hermès and Prada boutiques and the thirty-two-dollar brunch at Fred's that identify Chicago's Gold Coast as highly desirable urban real estate, a delightful assemblage of Stuff White People Like. Just down Division Street from the boutique hotels and the more-artisanal-than-thou Goddess and Grocer, Cabrini-Green is still in the early stages of gentrification, though it does have that universal identifier of urban reclamation: a Starbucks within view of another Starbucks.

All that remains of Cabrini-Green is sad stories and the original section of row houses around which the projects grew up. Those row houses are being renovated as part of the foundations-up effort to rebuild the neighborhood. Even the name "Cabrini-Green" is being scrubbed from memory: The new mixed-income development on the site of the old Cabrini-Green Extension heaves under the unbearably pretentious name

"Parkside of Old Town." But some of the old commerce remains, and Freckles is pretty clearly an entrepreneur of the street. "You buying?" I ask what he's selling, and he explains in reasonably civil terms that he is not in the habit of setting himself up for entrapment on a narcotics charge.

Cabrini-Green has had its share of tourists—in 1999, the film *Whiteboyz* showcased a group of Wonder Bread–colored hip-hop fans from Iowa visiting the site. But real estate and the scarcity thereof is the ruling fact of urban life, and once downtown Chicago began to evolve from a place where people work in factories and warehouses into a place where people work in law offices and university classrooms, Chicago's near north began to fill up with the sort of people who prefer urban lofts to suburban picket fences, public transit to car commutes, and thirty-two-dollar Sunday brunches to church, all of them living in the orbit of Cabrini-Green. Chicago is a very liberal place, but it's a very liberal place in which about half of the very liberal public-school teachers preach the virtues of the city's very liberal public schools while sending their own kids to old-fashioned private schools. Chicago may vote for the party of housing projects, but nobody wants to live next to one, or even drive past one on the way to Trader Joe's. One local tells of the extraordinary measures he used to take to avoid driving by Cabrini-Green, where children would pelt his car with bottles and trash whenever he stopped. Eventually he learned not to stop at all, blowing through red lights on the theory that it was better to risk a moving violation than risk what the locals might do to him.

So they tore down Cabrini-Green. And they tore down the Robert Taylor Homes and the Henry Horner Homes and practically every other infamous housing project in the city. And in doing so, Chicago inadvertently exacerbated the crime wave that now has the city suffering more than twice as many murders every year as Los Angeles County or Houston.

YOU CANNOT REALLY UNDERSTAND CHICAGO without understanding the careers of Larry Hoover, David Barksdale, and Jeff Fort, the three kings of the modern Chicago criminal gang. Chicago has a long history of crime syndicates, of course, including Al Capone and his epigones. In the 1950s it had ethnic street gangs of the *West Side Story* variety, quaint in pictures today with their matching embroidered sweaters and boyish names: the Eagles, the Dragons. But in the 1960s, marijuana began to change all that. Marijuana, that kindest and gentlest of buzzes, was a major money-making opportunity, both for the international syndicates that smuggled it and for the street criminals at the point of purchase. Inspired partly by Chicago's long mob history, partly by the nascent black-liberation ethic of the day, and a great deal by the extraordinary money to be made, Chicago's black gangs came to dominate the marijuana business—an enterprise model that would soon become supercharged by cocaine and heroin. David Barksdale built a tightly integrated top-down management structure for his gang, the Black Disciples, while Larry Hoover and Jeff Fort did the same thing for theirs, the Gangster Nation and the Black P-Stone Rangers, respectively. Barksdale and Hoover would later join forces as the Gangster Disciples, a group that, though faction-ridden, remains a key player on the Chicago crime scene today, with thousands of members—fifty-three of whom were arrested for murder in 2009 alone.

Fort had real organizational flair and transformed the P-Stones, a gang dating back to the 1950s, into one of the first true modern gangs, combining racialism, neighborhood loyalties, a hierarchical management structure complete with impressive-sounding titles, and the shallow self-help rhetoric of the 1960s into something new—holding the whole thing together with great heaping piles of money. His audacity was something to be wondered at: He formed a nonprofit organization and managed to convince city and federal officials that he was engaged in efforts to help disadvantaged urban youth. Government grant money was forthcoming, and soon the Gangster Disciples got in on the action, founding their own project called "Growth and Development"—note the initials. Bobby Gore and Alfonso Alfred of the rival Vice Lords secured a $275,000 grant from the Rockefeller Foundation. Like the Mafiosi of old, Chicago's new generation of gangsters recycled some of that money into political campaigns and the churches of influential ministers.

In fact, though they trafficked in narcotics and murder with equal ease, as often as not it was financial crimes ranging from misappropriation of federal money to mortgage fraud that brought down many of the top Chicago gangsters. Fort went to Leavenworth in the early 1970s for misuse of federal funds and continued to run his operations from federal custody until just a few years ago, when he was shipped off to the ADX Florence supermax lockup in Colorado and his communication with the outside world was severely curtailed. Hoover got two hundred years for murder and a life sentence for a federal narcotics charge but also continued to run his organization from prison.

Those government grants may not have amounted to very much, drops in the roaring river of money that the drug business was generating, but government contributed mightily to the growth of the modern gang by providing the one key piece of infrastructure that the Barksdales and Hoovers of the world could never have acquired for themselves: the high-rise housing project. The projects not only gave the gangs an easily secured place to consolidate their commercial activities, they also helped to create the culture of loyalty and discipline that was the hallmark of the Chicago street gang in its golden age. With most members living and working under the same roof, the leaders could quickly quash intra-gang disputes or freelance criminality. Fort, Hoover, and Barksdale were children of the 1940s and 1950s, men who came of age before the cultural rot of the 1960s—practically Victorians by the standards of the modern gangster. They were (and are) brutes and killers, but they managed to maintain some semblance of cohesion and structure. Barksdale went so far as to collect taxes—fees from unaffiliated drug dealers operating on his streets.

When the towers came down, Chicago's organized crime got a good deal less organized, and a number of decapitation operations run by the Chicago police and federal authorities had the perverse effect of making things worse: Where there once were a small number of gangs operating in a relatively stable fashion under the leadership of veteran criminals, today there are hundreds of gangs and thousands of gang factions.

Chicago police estimate that there are at least 250 factions of the Gang-ster Disciples alone, with as many as 30,000 members among them. Vast swathes of Chicago are nominally under the black-and-blue Disciples flag, but in reality there is at least as much violence between those Dis-ciples factions as between the Disciples and rivals. Some are one- and two-block operations, many with young teens in charge. The Barksdales and Hoovers may not have been Machiavellian in their subtlety, but they were far-seeing visionaries compared with the kids who came streaming out of the projects and took over the drug business in their wake.

MR. BUTT IS DEARLY MISSING HIS AK-47. He's a native of Pakistan, where Mikhail Kalashnikov's best-known invention is as common as the deer rifle is in the United States, but in Chicago he cannot possess even a peashooter, which has him slightly nervous in his role as my ghetto tour guide, chauffeuring me through the worst parts of Englewood and Garfield, the biggest battlegrounds in Chicago's twenty-first-century gangland warfare.

"In Pakistan, everybody has an AK-47," he says. "But it's not like here. They don't go walking into a school and shooting people." I ask him if he thinks that applies to the case of fifteen-year-old Malala Yousafzai, the Pakistani girl who was shot by Islamists for the crime of wanting to go to school. He allows that this is a fair point. He points out Bridgeport, home of the venerable Daley clan, and informs me wistfully that in the old days blacks simply were not allowed to cross the bridge into Bridgeport, a social norm enforced with baseball bats and worse. Mr. Butt is a big, big Daley fan—"He was very strong, strong with the mob!"—and no fan at all of Chicago's new breed of gangsters. "On the South Side, it is just like Afghanistan. Every square mile has its own boss, and everybody has to answer to him. From the business district through Thirty-First Street, everything is perfect." *Perfect* may not be the word, but I get his point. "Below Thirty-First Street, everything is jungle."

Mr. Butt locks the doors, and we cruise through Englewood and its environs. Martin Luther King Drive, like so many streets named for the

Reverend King, is a hideous dog show of squalor and dysfunction, as though Daniel Patrick Moynihan's depressing reportage in 1965's *The Negro Family* had been used as a how-to manual. Mr. Butt points out the dealers, who don't really need pointing out. It's about eight degrees Fahrenheit outside, and the Windy City is living up to its name. In the vicinity of Rothschild Liquors, grim-faced men in heavy coats smoke cigarillos and engage in commerce. Mr. Butt's habit of pointing out miscreants by literally pointing them out brings scowls from the street. Lying low is not Mr. Butt's strong suit.

Mr. Butt informs me that for many years the South Side dealers favored gas stations as bases of operation, which makes sense: Cars have a legitimate reason to be pulling in and out. Plausible deniability keeps probable cause at bay. Nobody is flying any obvious gang colors, no gold bandanas for the Four Corner Hustlers or crowns for the Latin Kings. But maybe that is simply because it is so god-awful cold and even the proudest gangster is bundled up. I've been told to look for Georgetown gear to identify the Gangster Disciples, but it may be that the Hoyas have become passé. Commerce is impossible to hide completely, however, and in truth it doesn't look like the locals are trying particularly hard to hide it. A maroon Cadillac sedan of Reaganite vintage comes slowly rumbling around the corner with four very serious-looking young men inside. Another young man in a heavy coat, carrying a plastic grocery bag that I suspect is full of commerce, comes out of a house to parley. Maybe they're talking about the weather, but probably not.

Mr. Butt takes me to see the sights: In front of Alexander Graham Bell Elementary School, there's commerce. On Garfield Boulevard, at Fifty-Eighth and Ashland, in front of the storefront churches, pawn shops, tax-refund-loan outlets, the mighty wheels of endless commerce roll on and on.

"They do this to their own neighborhood," Mr. Butt says, exasperated. "They make it a place no decent person would want to be. Why do they do that? It's very bad, very scary at night." This from a guy who vacations in Lahore.

Malala Yousafzai was a fifteen-year-old schoolgirl who got shot for a reason—a terrible, awful, evil reason, but a reason. (Say what you like about Islamic radicalism, at least it's an ethos.) All of Chicago is aghast at the story of fifteen-year-old Hadiya Pendleton, who was shot—and, unlike Malala Yousafzai, killed—apparently for no reason at all, at 2:20 in the afternoon in a public park. Miss Pendleton was a student at King College Prep and a majorette in the school's band, which had the honor of performing at Barack Obama's first inauguration. She had just recently returned from a trip to the president's second inauguration when she took shelter from the rain under a canopy at Harsh Park. Hadiya Pendleton was not known to have any gang connections—in fact, she had appeared in a 2008 video denouncing gang violence.

The shooting of Miss Pendleton commanded the attention of the White House and, naturally, that of President Obama's former chief of staff, Rahm Emanuel, now mayor of Chicago and fecklessly reshuffling the organization chart of the police department. The usual noises were made about gun control, and especially the flow of guns from nearby Indiana into Chicago, though nobody bothered to ask why Chicago is a war zone and Muncie isn't. But the mayor's latest promises did not impress seventeen-year-old Jordyn Willis, who organized a march in Miss Pendleton's memory. "He can't control his city," Miss Willis told the *Chicago Tribune*.

IT'S NOT CLEAR THAT ANYBODY CAN. Chicago has had three police superintendents since 2007. Current superintendent Garry McCarthy, formerly the head of the Newark police, has instituted the data-driven CompStat system first developed by the NYPD. But in a city in which fifteen-year-olds are running criminal enterprises and shooting each other over the slightest of slights, it's not clear that even the best policing practices will be sufficient.

"Some gangs require a shooting as part of the initiation," explains Art Bilek of the Chicago Crime Commission. Mr. Bilek is a wonderful anachronism, a very old-fashioned gentleman who uses the word "wisenheimer" without a trace of irony and refers to his former colleagues in the Chicago Police Department as "coppers." Now in his eighties, he joined the police force with a master's degree in hand at a time when it was unusual for a cop to have an undergraduate degree. He eventually rose to the rank of lieutenant in Chicago and chief of the Cook County sheriff's police, founding the academic discipline of criminal justice studies along the way.

"The purpose of tearing down the projects was to re-gentrify the neighborhoods. And now, where there had been projects, you have chain stores, exclusive restaurants, delis, everything people want. But it also sent those gangs out into the neighborhoods, into new places in the city and the suburbs, places where they had not been." He estimates that about 80 percent of Chicago's homicides are gang-related.

He sketches a pyramid. "In the old days, you had a Jeff Fort or a David Barksdale at the top of the pyramid. You had a very rigid structure, like the old Mafia, with a boss at the top, enforcers, and advisers. There was very strict enforcement of the rules—they'd beat you, maybe even kill you. And to an extent, the gangs could cooperate, because you had some structure. And you had it all going on in the projects, in those tall towers of criminality. And life was terrible for the people who had to live there. At the same time, you have a strong incentive to take those projects and do something else with them, to create revenue-producing lands—public housing pays no taxes. You can get rid of the towers, but the gangs that were in them don't just go away."

Worse, the move out of the projects has made it easier to bring juveniles into the gangs. "In the homes, they had a limited number of juveniles at any given time. Now, it's unlimited," he explains. "You have juveniles rising to positions of power, and they just don't have the street smarts or wisdom that even a Jeff Fort would. They're doing impulsive things that the old guard just wouldn't have dreamt of. And the money is bigger now, too. Before, the money went straight up to Hoover, Barksdale, or Fort, but now you have 1,000 leaders all competing for that. And you have the street gangs, the Mexican cartels, the narcotics, and the violence forming a unitary cultural phenomenon." He'd like to see stricter gun control and stiffer sentences—"burying them"—for violent offenders. He cites procedural changes in the legal system that make it more difficult to secure charges as a factor in the growing violence.

Chicago was the only U.S. city to break 500 murders last year, and that is a spike—but not an all-time high. Chicago has seen these spikes before: The city saw 516 murders in 2008, and it had nearly 1,000 in 1974, the year David Barksdale's past finally caught up with him and he died of kidney failure resulting from a gunshot wound suffered years before. Things have been worse in the past, but there is a sense that Chicago is moving in the wrong direction. New York City had nearly 2,000 murders in 1974, and more than 2,000 the year before. But those numbers are unthinkable today: New York City finally got control of itself, which is a big part of the reason why Rudy Giuliani, a thrice-married, recreationally cross-dressing, pro-choice, big-city liberal, was briefly taken seriously as a candidate for the Republican presidential nomination. Rahm Emanuel would need a miracle worthy of his surname to follow a similar path, to persuade Freckles to give up commerce and to get Mr. Butt to regard him as something other than a municipal joke.

Chicago may have torn down the projects, but building the city is a different thing altogether.

Screaming Man

Philadelphia

PHILLY IS FAMOUS FOR TWO THINGS: cheesesteaks and murder.

It's also well known for being—in Lincoln Steffens's classic phrase—"corrupt and contented." Philadelphia has one of the most backward and incompetent city governments in America, but its problems go beyond public administration. Philadelphia suffers from a combination of failed civic institutions, a deeply embedded racial paranoia that undermines law enforcement, and a local culture that shrugs at the urban chaos this produces. Philadelphia stands as a warning to other big American cities: This is how you drown under a crime wave.

In 2006, the one-or-two-a-day-and-a-dozen-on-weekends murder spree that earned "Killadelphia" its rap as an urban abattoir came to what everybody hopes was its guns-blazing peak, leaving 406 people dead. Another 392 were murdered in 2007. By way of comparison, Phoenix, which recently overtook Philadelphia as the nation's fifth-largest city, had 238 murders in 2006. San Antonio, a city nearly Philadelphia's size and sharing many of its economic challenges, had 119 murders. It's clearly not all about poverty: Miami, America's poorest major city, saw 79 homicides in all of 2006. In March 2006, more

Americans died violently on the streets of Philadelphia than died fighting in Iraq—and March wasn't the city's worst month of that year.

That Iraq comparison isn't made casually. In an August 2007 *Washington Post* article titled "The War in West Philadelphia," surgeon John P. Pryor described his experience this way: "In the swirl of screams and moving figures, my mind drifted to my recent experience in Iraq as an Army surgeon. There we dealt regularly with 'mascals,' or mass-casualty situations. In Iraq, ironically, I found myself drawing on my experience as a civilian trauma surgeon each time mascals would over-run the combat hospital. As nine or ten patients from a firefight rolled in, I sometimes caught myself saying 'just like another Friday night in West Philadelphia.'"

For the tourist, it must be hard to believe that all this mayhem is happening in the city where schoolchildren go to see the Liberty Bell and Carpenters' Hall. Center City, as Philadelphia's core is called, is vibrant, diverse, affluent, and full of cafés and theaters. Ten-year property-tax abatements encouraged a boom of condo conversions, and new skyscrapers transformed the city's skyline. Ed Rendell, mayor from 1992 to 2000, made attracting new business and investment to Center City the cornerstone of his mayoralty, and he still enjoys the reputation of a minor divinity in the city. But there was a hollowness to Rendell's achievement: Those skyscrapers became home to floors and floors of vacant or underutilized real estate. A wage tax of over 4 percent continued to drive the middle class out of the city and into the suburbs. Small and independent entrepreneurs, when they weren't being milked by union thugs, were suffocated under an expensive and complex tax regime. Rendell left Philadelphia with some of the worst public schools in the country, so incompetently run that the state had to take them over in 2001. And Rendell's final kick in the shins was leaving this mess in the hands of America's least competent mayor, John Street, who succeeded him in 2000.

The worst of Philadelphia's murder rampage corresponds roughly with the Street years, and it is not difficult to see why. Street's administration was a crime spree in its own right. Though the mayor was never charged with a crime, his inner circle kept prosecutors busy: The city treasurer was sentenced to ten years in prison on a twenty-seven-count federal corruption indictment and took a couple of bankers down with him, and the mayor's consigliere died before facing trial on similar charges. A prominent Muslim leader close to Street was convicted of using his political influence to win financial favors, while the mayor's brother, a hot-dog vendor (fronting a company with no employees) with no relevant experience to speak of was offered a no-bid million-dollar contract to provide services at the city's airport.

Politics constantly hobbles the ability of the city's capable police department to address crime. One illustrative episode involves the shooting of a sixteen-year-old student outside of Strawberry Mansion High School in West Philadelphia. The head of the school district went to the mayor pleading for more police patrols during the immediate after-school hours, which are the most dangerous time of day for students. But the proposal was scotched by Sandra Dungee Glenn, an African-American school-board member and former chief of staff to Representative Chaka Fattah. Glenn argued that deploying extra police in the area would send the wrong message to students and make them feel "that we need to be armed against them." Mayor Street chimed in that he wouldn't trust "a cop with a Glock" in the schools. So, for reasons of racial politics, black leaders, along with Philadelphia's black mayor and its black police chief, directed its heavily black police force to leave black students vulnerable to black criminals.

Sandra Dungee Glenn was subsequently named chair of the School Reform Commission. That's Philly.

The problem is that Sandra Dungee Glenn was right. Black neighborhoods in Philadelphia would feel under siege if they received the police attention they desperately need. As one Philadelphia cop put it, "I can solve crime in these neighborhoods tomorrow. You put a cop on every street corner. But the neighborhoods will complain, and the city won't pay for it."

The careers of mediocrities such as John Street and Sandra Dungee Glenn have been made possible by what might be called "the paranoid style in African-American politics," the elevation of racial loyalty over citizenship. The hogwash proffered by Barack Obama's mentor, the Reverend Jeremiah Wright—AIDS is a government plot to kill African Americans, the CIA peddles crack—is pretty mild compared to political discourse in black Philadelphia. Before the 2004 election, one black newspaper warned its readers to flee the city because President Bush was planning to suppress the inner-city vote . . . with nuclear weapons. This paranoid style is deeply embedded in the race-based politics of Philadelphia, and the police catch the worst of it.

"WE HAVE AN AVID HATE FOR THE POLICE," says Michelle Green, a black woman working an overnight shift near the Convention Center. "Black police officers have taken on the role of overseers," she says, smiling at the whip-cracking plantation metaphor. "They are haters of their own race." This attitude is not isolated. "Stop Snitchin'" T-shirts, advertising a philosophy that threatens death to those who cooperate with police—"Snitches get stitches, and get found in ditches"—are a hot item at street kiosks. A former prosecutor reports seeing a woman who planned to give a statement in the murder of her son being physically dragged out of a police car by her neighbors.

But it is precisely in the black neighborhoods that the police are most needed. Nine of Philadelphia's twenty-five police districts, mostly in black neighborhoods, account for two-thirds of the city's homicides. African Americans represent about 85 percent of the homicide victims and a similar proportion of the killers.

None of this is lost on Judge Jeffrey Minehart. He was the first judge to preside over the city's special "gun court"; he now spends almost all of his time hearing Philadelphia homicide cases. On the day of our interview he happens to be hearing the case of a convicted drug dealer charged with gun possession. The defendant is acting as his own attorney, and he's no Perry Mason. He has to be physically prompted to stand when the judge enters the room. But he has cut a deal: two to four years in lockup and two years of probation. He'll probably do the time in boot camp, and that time will probably be closer to two years than to four. It's a slap on the wrist, but everybody seems pleased with it except the guilty party. He is disappointed that his sentencing is immediate. "Do we have to do it *now*?" he asks.

This guy isn't the kind of armed felon who makes the news in Philadelphia. On the morning of Not-Perry-Mason's trial, the papers were full of the hunt for all-star fugitive Eric DeShawn Floyd, an armed robber with seventeen priors and a fondness for SKS semiautomatic rifles, one of which he and his crew had just used to murder Philadelphia police sergeant Stephen Liczbinski in the aftermath of a botched bank robbery. The man who actually pulled the trigger, Howard Cain, died in a shootout with police, but Floyd got away. Three men, disguised as burka-clad Muslim women, were involved in the heist. The *Philadelphia Daily News* carried an infographic describing the SKS with the headline: "Should This Gun Be Legal?" There was no *Daily News* headline asking why a felon with seventeen entries on his rap sheet was walking abroad in Philadelphia. Should that be legal?

It's a question that needs asking, but Philadelphia's news media, clergy, and civic leaders won't start that conversation. Two of the three Philadelphia police officers murdered over the past two years were killed by convicted criminals. Most cop killers have criminal histories. But the *Daily News*, like the rest of official Philadelphia, has learned the hard way that it's easier to blame remote lawmakers in Harrisburg or Washington than to take an honest look at Philadelphia's criminal realities. In 2002, the *Daily News* featured mug shots of fourteen fugitive murderers wanted in Philadelphia on its front page and ran pictures of twenty-seven more inside. Two of the fugitives were apprehended soon after their pictures were published, but the newspaper quickly found itself the subject of boycotts and protests because all of the fugitives whose pictures were published were black, Hispanic, or Asian. The *Daily News* didn't racially filter the photos: There simply weren't any white murder fugitives wanted in Philadelphia at that time. But the paper was nonetheless accused of racism, and some of its own staffers joined in the festival of denunciation. In the end, the newspaper knuckled under and apologized for publishing the truth. Shameful stuff.

Since then, the city's newspapers, like the district attorney, the mayors, and most of official Philadelphia, have found it much safer to blame Philadelphia's bloodshed on distant bogeymen in Congress and rednecks at the NRA. The city government isn't the only failed institution in Philadelphia.

Judge Minehart, too, argues for better gun control, but he is quick to admit that it wouldn't have stopped Howard Cain from murdering Sergeant Stephen Liczbinski with a stolen gun. Asked if he has ever seen a legally purchased firearm used in a crime, Judge Minehart looks surprised by the question. "For homicides, sure, though it's pretty rare. Outside of that . . . not that I can think of. Practically none." Which is to say, the gun control laws already on the books are so poorly enforced, or so unenforceable, that they are almost meaningless. This fact is not lost on Judge Minehart. "Gun control is a piece of the puzzle, I think, but it's only one piece of the puzzle," the judge says. "Drugs are a piece of the puzzle, too, but people overestimate how much of this homicide is drug-related. Corner fights and turf wars are probably about 30 percent. That's a big piece, sure, but it's not the largest. A strong percentage of these crimes are anger-related." Minehart is no bleeding-heart liberal, but he believes that intelligently administered anger-management therapy can prevent murders. Guns don't kill people—rage kills people.

Judge Minehart also argues that expanding the gun court over which he once presided could help cut into the crime. Gun-court cases are handled separately from the generality of criminal cases. The probation officers' caseloads are limited, and probationers are drug-tested twice a month. Philadelphia, a city of about 1.5 million, has some 50,000 people on probation. Outside of gun court, the typical Philadelphia probation officer has between 150 and 175 cases, making close monitoring impossible. If those probationers are drug-tested at all, it happens only once every six months.

But official Philadelphia cannot set intelligent priorities, and gun court is hobbled because the city cannot find an extra million or two in its bloated, patronage-packed $4 billion budget. Another program, Operation Safe Streets, put extra police officers on patrol in neighborhoods suffering the worst crime problems. But in true Philly style, the program was staffed through police overtime, which gets very expensive, instead of having its patrols built into regularly budgeted police duties.

The city's new mayor, Michael Nutter, is something different for Philadelphia: a squeaky-clean technocrat with a kind of nerdy anti-charisma. He is more given to low-key problem-solving than to displays of inspiring oratory. He has already taken some baby steps to set a few things right, including pulling 250 police officers from less pressing duties and putting them on patrol in high-crime areas. But it is far from clear that Nutter can do for Philadelphia what Rudy Giuliani did for New York. Nutter doesn't enjoy the same sort of princely powers that a New York mayor can muster, and there isn't going to be a stock-market boom to carpet Philadelphia with money the way Wall Street rained legal tender on Giuliani-era New York.

Philadelphia still has a bull market in murder, and it is far from clear that any political reform can change the culture of a city that has simply come to accept Third World levels of disorder and corruption.

A COUPLE OF YEARS AGO, *National Geographic* called Philadelphia "America's Next Great City." That motto is already fading on the side of a building near City Hall. Is Philadelphia on the road to recovery, like post-Giuliani New York—or is it more like Detroit? The indicators aren't good: Established businesses are fleeing, and they're being replaced by casinos, thanks to the efforts of Ed Rendell and John Street on behalf of the gambling lobby.

There is something strangely antique in Philadelphia's politics—its old-timey union bosses and unapologetic patronage, its sweetheart contracts for the mayor's brother. But what really makes an impression isn't the governmental incompetence, but the blasé acceptance of quotidian chaos on a scale that wouldn't be tolerated in New York, Atlanta, or Houston. Philly is what you get when you combine San Francisco crazy with Trenton's economy. Exhibit A: the raving homeless guy nicknamed Screaming Man, who comes careering out of an alley into ritzy Rittenhouse Row, ranting that he has AIDS and threatening to bite passersby. He screams, threatens, howls, and generally makes an urban spectacle of himself as diners at the nearby sidewalk cafes nibble on sixteen-dollar Gruyère cheeseburgers and drink espresso. He's been doing this shtick for years and years, without risking intervention from authority of any kind or even really commanding the attention of the rich guys coming out of Holt's Cigars, who just step around him as if he were dogshit. He's part of the local color, like incompetent mayors and Stop Snitchin' T-shirts, like leaving schoolkids vulnerable to criminals so as not to "send the wrong message."

Philadelphia's City Hall, perhaps America's most beautiful municipal building, is crowned with a statue of William Penn. But it might as well be Eric DeShawn Floyd or John Street, Not-Perry-Mason or Screaming Man: This is their city.

Play to Extinction

Atlantic City, New Jersey

W E ARE THE SILVER HORDE, and we are descending—on chartered buses, on Chinatown buses, and on the Greyhound "Lucky Streak" express bus we come, on crutches and canes, lapping obesely over the seats of mobility scooters, adjusting oxygen tubes, discreetly nursing Big Gulp cups full of tequila and Pepsi through bendy straws at three in the afternoon, doing serious damage to complimentary troughs of Cheez-Its and Famous Amos cookies. We are getting *comped*. Free passes to the all-you-can-eat buffet? What*ever*. We have our own dedicated *train*, Amtrak's Atlantic City Express Service (read: ACES), and we come rolling and thundering down the tracks bearing our Social Security checks, our welfare checks, and quite possibly our rent checks. We are the blue-rinsed, unhinged, diabetic American id on walkers, and we are scratching off lottery tickets the whole way there as we converge from all points on the crime capital of New Jersey—because *we are feeling lucky*.

Funny thing about Atlantic City: Nobody feels really obviously lucky to *live* there. Its population is declining (40 percent off since its peak), and among the foot soldiers of the gambling industry—blackjack dealers, scantily clad cocktail waitresses, cab drivers—it is difficult to find anybody who actually lives there. One lightly clothed entertainer working at a

particularly gamey establishment along a row of empty commercial buildings, video stores, and the occasional storefront mosque—all within a
couple minutes' walk of the casino district—snorted derisively at the notion
of living in the city. "Oh, *hell* no. Too dangerous." That's AC: it's a great
place for a visiting go-go dancer, but she wouldn't want to live there. Tour-
ing the local landscape of decay and disorder, it is hard to imagine why a
whole range of American politicians—from such likely suspects as Ed
Rendell and Andrew Cuomo to lots of otherwise conservative Republicans
who really ought to know better—look at the city's depressed and depressing precincts, its sad coat of glitz (SINBAD! AT THE TROPICANA!) and say
to themselves: "My state needs to get some of *that* action!"

They had better think twice about what they are getting themselves
into. The issue of gambling is not a question of rah-rah libertarians versus
no-no bluestockings: Nobody who looks seriously at the nexus between
politics and gambling could possibly conclude that what is happening in
Atlantic City, in Pennsylvania, on the Indian reservations, or in the lottery
racket represents the operation of the free market. It is a cartel in most
cases, and a monopoly in many, all with the blessings of the state. The
arrangement, in the words of one scholarly study of casinos in Montana,
leaves government "a dependent partner in the business of gambling." If
gambling advocates were simply making a principled case that putative
adults have the right to entertain themselves with their own money according to their own tastes (or, let's be serious, lack thereof), then their argument might be persuasive. But what is in fact happening is that politicians
smell money, and so government itself is getting into the game, taking
gambling to be a fruitful model of economic development.

While the data are hotly contested, it is hard to deny that gambling
has taken more out of Atlantic City than Atlantic City has taken out of
gambling. A report prepared by the California Research Bureau on the
potential for gambling in that state found that while many of the AC
casinos had done well, there was little secondary economic impact: "The
success of gambling in Atlantic City," the report finds, "has done little
to revitalize the rest of Atlantic City and its business community. Atlantic

City has been described as two cities. One is the casinos, and the other is a city of boarded-up buildings with an unemployed minority work force. Gambling has largely failed in achieving the objectives of job growth for local residents and city-wide economic development."

The federal government's National Gambling Impact Study Commission notes that while gambling advocates favorably cite the "Mississippi Miracle," the economic boomlet that that state experienced after legalizing casino gambling, "in reality the unemployment rate in Mississippi declined at about the same rate as the national average in the years from 1992 to 1998." A University of Chicago report found that there was "no change in overall per capita income" as the result of gambling liberalization in the cases it studied. Governments, always eager to out-Enron Enron in the accounting-shenanigans Olympics, earmark gambling proceeds for popular programs, then reduce general-revenue support for those programs and use the extra money to increase spending elsewhere. It's a lot like slot machines: The house exploits the occasional jackpot to distract the schmucks from the fact that losses are a statistical inevitability. And while the accounting gets pretty hairy, it's not too hard to find entries on the losing side of the ledger: In one study of Atlantic City, 22 percent of the local homeless reported that gambling was the proximate cause of their condition.

YOU WOULDN'T KNOW THAT FROM THE VENTISOMETHINGS. They're the young ladies' auxiliary to the SILVER HORDE, climbing leggily out of Lamborghinis and GT-Rs in front of Borgata, and they are a tribe apart: stiletto heels with jeans, the inevitable Starbucks venti cup, Marlboro Light contrails. Borgata is by most accounts the swankiest place in Atlantic City, which tells you a lot about Atlantic City, because Borgata is a dump, albeit a kind of expensive one. It has some dimly lit nightclubs for the ventisomethings to frolic in, and it's big on overpriced restaurants serving food that was trendy ten years ago (Kobe burgers, Asian fusion), the kind of place that has architectural spaces meant to be imposing but a maintenance schedule that's running a bit behind: oversized glass showers and stained carpets. It's a mind-jarring mix, a lot of polished marble and women in stylish dresses, with something in the middle that resembles nothing so much as a Chuck E. Cheese's full of septuagenarians with mobility impairments. (Seriously, visit around 4:00 p.m.: It's wheelchair derby in there.) Unlike the relatively cheery Caesars in Vegas, which gold-leafs every surface with an inch of kitsch in a winking acknowledgement of the underlying plebeianness of the venue, Borgata affects a kind of Parisian hauteur like a down-on-his-luck aristocrat expecting things to get worse, which is what it is: In February it reported declining revenues and a 7 percent drop in operating profits. Gaming-industry analysts are gloomy about its outlook as the new $2.4 billion Revel casino prepares to open its doors.

For that new competition, Borgata can offer its gratitude to the great state of New Jersey and to Governor Chris Christie, thanks to whom taxpayers will be partners in, among other things, a burlesque show at Revel called "Royal Jelly." (The burlesque show will not be the only source of eye candy: The casino also is implementing some unusual business practices, including a plan to fire all of its servers, hostesses, and waitresses every four or six years and force them to reapply for their jobs, in a more-nakedly-brutal-than-usual strategy for weeding out anybody who doesn't look good in tall heels and a short skirt.) Revel began as a project headed up by the hapless Morgan Stanley, which owned 90 percent of the partnership behind the casino. In 2010 the bailed-out investment bank, facing bigger problems and unimpressed by recent Atlantic City revenues, took a billion-dollar write-down and pulled the plug on the half-finished project. Governor Christie moved in with a $261 million bailout of the orphan casino the bailed-out bank had bailed out on. Some of that money will be used for construction and operating expenses, but $70 million will sit quietly in an account earmarked for the project's new Wall Street financiers, so that they'll have something to walk away with if the casino tanks.[1]

Governor Christie had better hope it doesn't. In February he released a budget proposal that contains some implausibly optimistic financial projections: Among other things, he's betting that gambling revenues are going to rise by 14 percent, or nearly a half-billion dollars, resulting in $40 million in new taxes. While Governor Christie is putting up taxpayers' money for Revel, he can at least say he's getting government out of the way: There was a bloodbath at the Casino Control Commission, which was cut from 260 regulators and staff to 65, its budget reduced from $24 million to $9 million. (Taxpayers have little reason to celebrate that development: The commission's budget is funded largely by fees charged to casino operators, not by state taxes.) Lest some of those axed regulators end up on New Jersey's unemployment rolls, the state has been merrily signing waivers allowing them to go to work for the casinos, which they are forbidden by law to do for two years after leaving the commission. Governor Christie is executing what amounts to a state-level takeover of Atlantic City's gaming district, and he is, as they say, all in. His optimism is not shared by many gambling-industry analysts, including Deutsche Bank Securities managing director Andrew Zarnett, who says that he fears the project will not produce any new revenues: "Revel casino will mostly cannibalize existing operators," he told the *Press of Atlantic City*.

Which is to say, the supply of ventisomethings is limited. There's only so much play at the top of the market, but that's not where all the action resides, and the question that is seldom asked is: If New Jersey is successful in increasing its casino revenues, and Pennsylvania is successful, and Indiana is successful, and Mississippi is successful, and the Indians are successful, and Connecticut is successful—where exactly does the money come from?

The money will come from the SILVER HORDE. Casinos have long loved the high rollers, and the whales still rule in Vegas, but the low rollers are the new bread and butter for casinos in the rest of the country. If the politicians have their way, the SILVER HORDE will not have to hop on the *Lucky Streak* and go to Atlantic City: Atlantic City is coming to them.

HAVING LONG SINCE SHAKEN OFF THE LAST VESTIGES of its ancestral Quaker sobriety, Pennsylvania has opened up casinos everywhere from obscure Pittsburgh suburbs to Valley Forge, right near the monument to George Washington's brutal winter there, and the state flirted with licensing one on the edge of the battlefield at Gettysburg (the legal wrangling over it continues). The Gettysburg project was stopped because its opponents included people with some real money and influence, but money and influence are not evenly distributed, which is why there's a Harrah's casino in Chester, one of Pennsylvania's poorest cities (per capita income $9,052) and its most murder-happy (24 homicides in 2010 among 33,972 residents), a place where the school district just plain ran out of money in January, requiring a state bailout.

There's a lot of broke to go around: In a particularly depressing sign of the times, the parent company of the struggling *Miami Herald* sold the paper's Biscayne Bay headquarters to the Malaysian conglomerate Genting, which, in addition to its plantations and oil-and-gas businesses, is one of the world's largest gambling concerns. Genting is the largest casino operator in the United Kingdom, and it is expanding remorselessly in the United States. The Pequot tribe may be the name on the brass plate at the giant Foxwoods Resort in Connecticut, but it was Genting, through its Kien Huat Realty subsidiary, that put the money up for the project. The same with the Seneca Indians' casino at Niagara Falls and the Wampanoags' development in Massachusetts. Kien Huat Realty is the controlling shareholder in the Monticello Raceway in the Catskills, and Genting built the casino at the Aqueduct Racetrack in New York City.

Interestingly, Genting also has the contract to build the new New York City convention center—conveniently located next door to its casino in Queens. (Seriously—New York thinks America is coming to visit *Queens*.) Among Genting's demands for the project is that it be given a monopoly on video-poker licenses in the area. It's also asking for a sweeter revenue-sharing deal with the state and says that an amendment to New York State's constitution, which forbids table games and many other kinds of gambling, would be welcome. Governor Cuomo has pronounced himself favorably disposed, which puts him at odds with a long line of legendary New York politicians opposed to state-sanctioned gambling, from Fiorello La Guardia to Governor Cuomo's own father. (The Little Flower, who made a name for himself cracking down on gambling dens in 1930s New York—and smashing their paraphernalia with a sledgehammer—must be shaking his fist eternally in heaven that the city's first legal casino is a stone's throw from the horrifying airport named after him.)

When Genting showed up in Florida, it had plenty of cash to acquire the *Herald* building and surrounding properties, and it had plans in hand for a massive casino development. Which was pretty cocky, considering that casinos were not yet legal in Miami. "Nobody had even introduced a bill yet," says Paul Davies, a fellow at the Institute for American Values who runs a project called Get Government Out of Gambling. "Talk about thinking you've got it all sewn up." Genting hadn't counted on the intensity with which its project would be opposed by the Walt Disney Company, and the Miami casino bill died in the Florida legislature. The state chamber of commerce and the local hotel association and Indian gambling interests were opposed, too, along with a few political activists, but it was Mickey Mouse who killed the casinos—for now. "Those guys will be back," Davies says. And not only will they be back in Miami, they'll be back everywhere.

Dave Jonas, president of the Parx casino, which is nestled among the strip malls of the hideous Philadelphia suburb of Bensalem, offered a preview of coming attractions at a recent speech to the Pennsylvania gaming association (held at Valley Forge, hooray), in which he said his firm had "underestimated significantly" how often the locals would pop in to gamble: "When I was in Atlantic City, to have twelve to fifteen trips out of customers, they were VIPs," he said. At Parx, the low rollers are coming in two or three times a week, or 150 to 200 trips a year. "We have customers who give us $25, $30 five times a week." They call these local-yokel joints "convenience casinos," and they are the future: gambling anywhere, anytime. Some casinos are already experimenting with handheld devices so that players can piss their money away while actually in the bathroom.

THE INDUSTRY TERM OF ART that denotes success vis-à-vis any individual gambler is "PLAY TO EXTINCTION." The goal is to keep gamblers tied to the machines until they have handed over all the money they have to hand over. There are a great many ways to do this, but one way to keep the grannies tethered to the *Sex and the City: Change of a Dress* video slot machine is to keep them *literally* tethered: Casinos have begun offering rewards cards that give gamblers points based on their volume of play. The cards are affixed to neck lanyards and have to be kept plugged in to the machine to accrue points, creating a strangely umbilical sight.

The statistics are astounding: Gambling rates for the sixty-five-and-up demographic went from 35 percent in 1975 to 80 percent in 1990. By 1996, gambling was a bigger business than movies, recorded music, sports, live entertainment, and cruise ships—*combined*. And while there is a great deal of debate about gambling addiction and its role in the casino industry's business model, a government study found that "disordered gambling" rates are double for populations living within fifty miles of a casino. If cancer rates were double in the fifty miles surrounding a bubblegum factory, you can bet that the bubblegum factory would get the full Erin Brockovich treatment.

And it's not just the gambling rates: In the years after the first casinos were built, Atlantic City went from having the fiftieth-highest per capita crime rate in the United States to being number one on the list. That's a big price to pay, but many in government are willing to pay it—for a big enough cut of the action.

"The nanny state is bad news," Davies says. "But when you start looking into gambling and what the companies do, they're not just running a business. The more problematic part is the government's role. It's a joint venture between the government and the casinos, and gaming pays a higher tax rate than do other businesses. In Pennsylvania, slot-machine revenue is taxed at 55 percent rate—55 percent of the cut. Government is not a minority partner, but a majority partner."

The ride home on the Greyhound on Sunday morning is a damn sight less rollicking than the one down. A woman in the bus terminal is negotiating with a friend for a ticket home—she doesn't have enough money left on her ATM card to buy it, and she's pushing a handful of sweaty singles and loose change at her traveling companion. (Weird fact: You can use a card to get cash advances out of casino ATMs without entering a PIN—paradise for pickpockets.)

THE SILVER HORDE IS GETTING SOBER, and some are just plain sleeping it off, sprawled across seats and falling shambolically into the aisle. One woman is arguing on the phone with a third party who apparently has failed in her assigned duty to pick the lady's grandkids up from wherever they are staying. (The Parx in Bensalem has seen several gamblers cited for leaving their kids in parked cars while trying their luck inside.) Various byzantine personal and financial disputes are underway. One cannot help but recall the fact that between October 2009 and May 2010 some $1.8 million in California welfare benefits was withdrawn at casino ATMs; the corresponding Social Security figure must be shocking. The ventisomethings are off to Aspen or Mustique or wherever is in fashion this year. The SILVER HORDE is filing off grumpily at the Port Authority Bus Terminal and at Greyhound stations across the country, sad and bedraggled and losers right down to the literal Webster's meaning of the word. Cash has changed hands, but only in what economist Paul Samuelson called the "sterile transfers of money or goods between individuals, creating no new money or goods. Although it creates no output, gambling does nevertheless absorb time and resources. When pursued beyond the limits of recreation, where the main purpose after all is to 'kill time,' gambling subtracts from the national income." Call gambling a vice, call it an addiction, call it a harmless diversion, call it anything you fancy—but don't call it economic development.

Topless Chick, Uncredited

Vegas, Baby

"**E**GGS ARE EXPENSIVE, SPERM ARE CHEAP." That's a plain-English approximation of Bateman's principle: In a species with two sexes, the members of the sex that invests less biologically in reproduction will end up competing, sometimes ferociously, over the members of the sex that invests more. Because healthy men can, in theory, reproduce almost without limit while women are constrained by the number of pregnancies that they can take to term in a lifetime, women have a strong incentive to be more selective about their sexual partners, while men don't: snipers versus shotguns, basically. In a 2004 paper under the forthright title "Sexual Economics: Sex as Female Resource for Social Exchange in Heterosexual Interactions," two scholars from the University of British Columbia and Florida State took that insight and examined mating behavior through the lens of market competition. And if you doubt for one second that the pitiless laws of supply and demand provide an excellent explanation of human sexual behavior, then by all means make a reservation at the Hard Rock Hotel and Casino for the annual awards ceremony hosted by *Adult Video News*, also known as the "Porn Oscars," the most mercilessly Darwinian sexual marketplace you will find this side of Recife.

The awards show itself is almost an afterthought on the agenda of this multiday pornopalooza, which is one part serious insider trade show for the nation's increasingly specialized pornographers and sex-toy peddlers—Doctor Clockwork's Home for Electrical and Medical Oddities draws a curious crowd, as do the live product demonstrations, including one of a "sexercise" device that is basically one of those Sit 'N' Bounce balls we all had as kids, but with one or two additions—and one part fan-fest for the world's most dedicated consumers of smut, men who travel great distances and shell out hundreds of dollars in order to pack sweatily into crowded rooms and wait in line for autographs from their favorite performers, representing such powerhouses of porn production as Evil Angel, Morally Corrupt, and Brazzers, while manufacturers of sundry sexual devices and what one entrepreneur refers to bluntly as "dick pills" hawk their latest wares and potions at cheery display booths.

It is raw consumerism, and there's a kind of eerie symmetry at work: sex toys laid out in glass cases like jewelry at Tiffany's, women displayed like flank steaks at Safeway. Bateman's principle predicts that among primates like us, males will have a more lopsided distribution of sexual outcomes than will females: Basically all of the healthy females who survive to adulthood will have the opportunity to mate, but some of the males will be crowded out of the marketplace by a relatively small number of highly successful competitors—they just don't have the biological capital to compete in the Hobbesian sexual war of all against all. The guys buying VIP passes here at the Porn Oscars, sitting slack-jawed at Sapphires Gentlemen's Club as the performers swan through the crowd performing what is no doubt contractually required fan stroking, and then perhaps making a furtive or not-so-furtive trip down the highway to one of Nevada's legal brothels—these frustrated, cow-eyed men are Bateman's losers, and they are legion. The unkind industry term for them: *trenchcoats*.

On day one, the line of trenchcoats waiting to hand over $80 to $120 for a one-day pass to the event stretches from the box office well inside the Hard Rock across much of the length of the enormous casino past the bell desk and to the front door. Some of them are normal-guy "Vegas, Baby" tourists, and even couples out on a lark, but some of them aren't simply stopping by this circus on their way to Circus Circus: For them, this is the main event. They speculate among themselves about which of their favorites will be here this year and debate which performers and events they should visit first—like the Smithsonian, you can't see it all in one day, and you probably would invite some sort of retinal-glandular damage if you tried. One gentleman talks wistfully about Lisa Ann, a performer in the "mature" segment of the market whose career was revived by a timely impersonation of Sarah Palin—she's the Tina Fey of porn. The trenchcoats are young and old—a few old enough and decon-ditioned enough to require mobility scooters—and mostly white, though not exclusively so, their troglofaunal complexions suggesting a great deal of time spent awake in the dark. The contrast between the bearded, roly-poly trenchcoats and the performers—many of them tiny and fragile-looking, their massive surgical enhancements slung on slight avian frames in many cases barely five feet tall—calls to mind H. G. Wells: the Morlocks are here to consume the Eloi.

What's remarkable about the expo is just how square and corporate and conventional a trade show it is. Sure, there are a lot more impossibly pneumatic bare breasts displayed on the show floor than at your typical laundry-detergent convention, but that's just trenchcoat bait, and such lewdness as there is is drearily predictable. (Everybody sniggers in unison when an elevator emblazoned with the seriously curvaceous image of one Stormy Daniels announces: "Going down." Everybody, that is, except for one Rexxx Holz of Decadent D Digital, who is off in his own little apparently Stoic world.) Inside, in the sessions the gawkers are kept care-fully out of, there's a great deal of concern about whether the FDA—"three little letters with a whole shitstorm of stuff behind them," as the moderator puts it—is going to intervene in the herbal male-enhancement market, about inconsistent overseas regulation of benzocaine levels in penis desensitizers, about the high cost (up to $20,000) of getting FDA sign-off on particular blends of personal lubricants, and so forth.

Craig—he's just Craig, no surname, like Madonna or Sting but a known player in the sexual-products industry—complains that he could "rebuild a rain forest with all the paperwork I have," an observation met with general commiseration by the other panels in the regulation session. "We definitely don't have a sex-positive agent at the FDA, to say the least," complains one, and another declares, "The FDA has two jobs. One is to protect the consumer, and the other is to protect Big Pharma." They mirthfully deride FDA communiqués that quote Wikipedia articles on the subject of penis diameter, missives received in the course of the agency's leaning on them about certain vascular-constriction devices that the industry insists are "novelties" but the FDA considers "medical devices." They sound like coal executives discussing the EPA. While the trenchcoats are busy with the titillating displays outside, the industry operators are hearing pitches from logistics companies, legal advisers, cosmetic dentists, and bankers specializing in the unique challenges of the skin trade.

There's a strange sentimentality detectable here, too. There is a panel on the future of the feature-length porn film and a great deal of wistfulness about its decline. Attendees speak about the "golden age" of the 1970s, when porn movies lasted ninety minutes and had something resembling plotlines. People become distinctly uncomfortable when I inquire as to what exactly is the point of a ninety-minute porn film, given the use to which such films are habitually put. Later, I do a quick analysis of the clips offered at PornHub—one of the web's Big Three porn sites, along with RedTube and YouPorn—and calculate the average length of a clip at just under thirteen minutes.

Las Vegas is the perfect venue for the porn industry, which until the day before yesterday was dominated by California. Smut isn't the only business fleeing the politico-economic orbit of Sacramento, but its shift has been especially dramatic. After Los Angeles County passed a law mandating the use of condoms in pornographic films, applications for permits to produce them crashed by 95 percent—an industry group ran a series of humorous advertisements offering performers in full hazmat gear as a glimpse of the porn future—and with the San Fernando Valley sidelined, Vegas is picking up the slack. Like gambling, porn has its roots in the shadowy, semi-legal-to-outright-outlaw enterprises that still intersected with the edges of organized crime long after the high-water mark of the traditional criminal syndicates. And like slot machines and poker, porn has gone mainstream and corporate. The men conducting business on the sidelines of the AVN trade show are not in the main of the gold-chains-on-hairy-chest variety; they're your classic California entertainment-industry types, sandy-haired and looking like they have a lot invested in egg whites, personal trainers, and depilatory treatments. The corporate speak—"monetize," "brand-building," and so forth—is relentless.

"The days of just churning out product and selling DVDs are long gone," says director Miles Long, a two-time AVN award–winner with some fifty AVN nominations on his curriculum vitae—an honest-to-God official member of the AVN Hall of Fame. (I do not ask whether "Miles Long" is a nom de porn or an aptronym or what.) "Most of the revenue streams are internet-based, and we have to have multiple revenue streams: overseas, broadcast, DVD distribution, selling toys. The industry really failed to see the relevance of the internet, and it cost them." Mr. Long sounds positively Republican on the subject of California and Los Angeles County—"They are making it difficult for people to do business, with the insane taxes and regulations"—and on the virtues of his newly adopted hometown of Las Vegas: "It's Second Amendment–friendly, and there's no state income tax."

Poor feckless California: It can't even do porn right.

Elsewhere, a young entrepreneur speaks admiringly of Walmart's famous inventory-and-logistics system, which puts before customers products that they don't know that they want (the classic example being to stock bananas in the dairy aisle, since cereal buyers are likely to be banana buyers as well). "People on the internet are very focused when it comes to their masturbation," he says. "They know exactly what they want to be looking at." Pornographers have responded by carefully tracking what customers watch and what they search for, in order to connect them with ever more finely tailored content. Porn has, of course, long been a driver of technology. Two young webcam performers speak admiringly about a particularly considerate host company's IP-blocking technology. "If you have family in Texas, you can block anybody from Texas from logging in and seeing you," one says. It's a way to keep her career "private." People talk a great deal about privacy in this business; nobody talks about shame.

The market for porn is necessarily as unpredictable as the human sexual urge, and the near-uniformity of the performers is broken up by the occasional outlier: a three-hundred-pound woman in a fishnet top lounges near the pool. The possibility for finer and finer slicing of the market is being explored by Customs4U, a firm whose name and logo encircle my neck, being helpfully printed on the lanyards for press badges. Rather than having customers seek out the preexisting images they desire, this service allows them to go to the site, choose the performers they want and the scenarios they want, and have a bespoke porn clip sent to them for a fee that varies according to the length and unique demands of the film. "Girls with webcams do live shows, and there are clips for sale," says Kelly Shibari, who is manning the Customs4U booth. "What we do is we make the process efficient. They don't shoot a video until there has been an order." Customers can choose from a menu of scenarios, she explains, "or submit a script of their own. If you want a five-minute trampoline clip, that's what you get." (Given the alacrity with which the word "trampoline" enters the conversation, my impression is that this is not merely a hypothetical.) A relatively new enterprise, only three months in Customs4U has five hundred models doing as many as five to ten bespoke porn videos per week.

As specific as that tailored porn can be, the sex business still wants to come off the screen and into the world, a fact that comes into very sharp focus as A-list porn star Kaylani Lei totters past a life-sized Kaylani Lei sex surrogate manufactured by Realdoll, the Rolls Royce of inflatable girlfriends. A normal human being generally cannot walk past a mirror without taking a subconscious glance at it, but judging by outward appearances, Miss Lei is not a normal human being. I briefly consider asking her what it is like to be cast in high-quality plastic as a recreational masturbation aid, until I realize that the question is based on a rapidly vanishing distinction. With her surgical augmentations jutting out perpendicularly, as though resting on an invisible shelf, the main physical difference between Miss Lei and the sex-doll version of her is the percentage of artificial filler. These trenchcoats are not here for reality—the aftermarket parts are the point. Porn is no longer an ersatz, last-option sexual substitute—it is an end unto itself. The AVN spectacle turns out to be a perverse vindication of the theories of Jacques Lacan: The signifier here has indeed taken precedence over the thing signified.

But technology has not yet brought us to the place where digital pornography is entirely immersive, and so the Las Vegas sex trade remains an unholy trinity of porn, strip clubs, and the studiously-not-talked-about (at least at AVN) legal brothels down the road. Prostitution remains formally illegal in Las Vegas, though as everywhere the rise of the internet and mobile communication has made policing it practically impossible. But legal prostitution is just an hour away and a county over, and the enterprising brothel owners of Nevada are more than happy to dispatch a limousine to any Las Vegas destination and ferry clients across the relevant county lines.

I DON'T EVEN BOTHER putting the coordinates of the Chicken Ranch into my phone; I assume, incorrectly, as it turns out, that when I cross into Pahrump, Nevada—unofficial municipal motto: "WHERE THINGS GO PAH-RUMP IN THE NIGHT!"—I will be greeted by billboards, if not a thicket of flashing neon signs, reading "WHORES THIS WAY!" Instead there's the usual southwestern sprawl, the fifty-shades-of-beige Nevada landscape punctuated by little rectangles of Pantone 342 green giving way to Carl's Jr. and Walmart. The only sign of the sex traffic is the literal traffic, which includes a suspiciously large number of black Lincoln Town

Cars. You take a left at the local strip club, drive down Homestead Road past the Heritage Bible Church and the Second Missionary Baptist Church, cross the unambitiously named Thousandaire Boulevard, upon which sits a combination casino and RV park, pass the Ten Commandments plaque affixed to a utility pole, and only then do you see two discreet signs, each no more than eighteen inches across, one advertising the famous Chicken Ranch, the other advertising its next-door competitor, Sheri's Ranch. You are right on top of them before there's significant signage.

The two establishments are quite similar, though Sheri's has a reputation as the slightly more upscale member of the pair. The Chicken Ranch is faux Wild West Victorian, while Sheri's appears to be a converted motel. Both are decorated in a combination of old-fashioned men's club and modern suburban sports bar. Sheri's has overnight accommodations for those so inclined. You can go in, order a drink, mingle with such commodities as are available, or call for a "line-up," which is exactly what it sounds like. Fees are charged by specific service, not by time, and negotiations can be excruciatingly detailed. The shy can make these arrangements by telephone or email in advance, to avoid the embarrassing possibility of being told to your face that you have made a request that a prostitute is unwilling to fulfill.

Prices are pretty high at these establishments—you can spend more than $1,000 easily—but they are less than what you're going to spend for three nights at the Hard Rock Hotel and three days' worth of VIP passes for the porno expo. And there's actual sex to be had. Not only sex, but sex with porn stars—J. R. Carrington, who appeared in more than a hundred porn films, is listed on the current Chicken Ranch roster. (IRONY ALERT: She once appeared in a film called *Whorehouse*.) For porn fans considering a brothel trip, there's some ugly statistics-and-probability work to do: Nevada's legal prostitutes are screened for HIV and other venereal diseases every thirty days; the current best practice in the porn business is to screen performers every fourteen days. Like California's porn performers, Nevada's prostitutes are legally required to use condoms. But the thought of sex with somebody professionally obliged to undergo HIV screening twelve or twenty-six times a year is a powerful dysaphrodisiac. I notice that the housekeeper tidying up the overflowing ashtrays in the lobby at the hotel this week is wearing black hygienic gloves that match her uniform.

BACK AT THE HARD ROCK, things are pulsing. A middle-aged Asian man looking for all the world like he's going to a costume party as Ken Jeong's character in *The Hangover*—shiny red suit over a tacky print shirt, the checkerboard pattern on his Louis Vuitton loafers matching his man-purse—bobs and snaps to music heard only by himself while he waits for the valet. The AVN line is back out to the door again, and go-go dancers have been stationed at the venue entrance as trenchcoat appetizers. Ron Jeremy, who is basically Clint Eastwood in this milieu, chats quietly in the hallway with a small knot of men, his pop-eyed hypertensive face seemingly lit from within by an unwholesome radiance. Down the hall, a tired middle-aged exhibitor sits in the pop-up café sponsored by Wicked Pictures, counting out the day's medication from prescription-drug bottles lined up neatly on the table in front of him. Milling about are representatives of the XXX Church, a seriously mixed-message outfit whose porn-mustache-and-palm-trees logo and glib messaging—"JESUS LOVES PORN STARS"—belie its serious concern about porn addiction. Its porn-and-pancakes breakfast discussion is wedded to a thirty-days-porn-free challenge.

I am introduced to Nikki Phoenix—the number of "X"s in her surname is variable; I've seen as many as three—who is a nominee this year in the category of best "crossover" performer. "Crossover" denotes a performer who does "mainstream" work as well as porn, and Miss Phoenix—who has family in Phoenix—has appeared in non-porn offerings from billboard campaigns to not-quite-porn men's magazines to the immediately forgotten comedy *21 and Over*, with the IMDb page listing her as "Topless Chick, Uncredited."

As Miss Phoenix tells it, porn—and the billboards and the lad mags and the lingerie modeling—is an exercise in living well as the best revenge. She is not planning to title her memoir *Topless Chick, Uncredited*. From her point of view, hers is a story of triumph in the face of adversity. An early bloomer who developed breasts well before most of her peers and then became seriously overweight, Miss Phoenix was tormented by bullies whose abuse ran the entire gamut from mean-girl insults—she was nicknamed "Sandwich"—and social exclusion to more serious stuff, including outright violence. Being relegated to remedial reading classes did not help. (For all you former tormented nerds out there, remember what high school was like and then add to that the humiliation and hopelessness of being an academic underperformer.) There were even darker experiences outside of school. She eventually completed a vocational course and dropped out of high school to work in a veterinarian's office, and life began to improve slowly. Eventually she lost 120 pounds, began posting photos of her newly slender self on Facebook, and in time was approached by a porn producer. After her first scene, she says, she was "hooked." Doing porn was "the epitome of everything I wasn't." Her parents have been supportive of her career. "My family is very liberal," she says. "My mom says she'd do it if she could. My dad just says that I've ruined Google for him." The Goldwater-country branch of her family, which she describes as "Republican and conservative," is less enthusiastic, and the extended family's *modus vivendi* is an agreement not to talk about it.

She is writing a diet book under the working title *Fit as Phoenix*. Every performer here seems to be writing a book: porn actress Asa Akira advertises her forthcoming memoir, *Porn: A Love Story*, to be brought out by the same house that publishes P. J. O'Rourke: "The world has seen every fold of my most private parts, and yet I feel this book is my most exposing venture yet." Such are the demands of maintaining multiple revenue streams.

Having transformed herself from fat to merely buxom and garnered an AVN nomination, Miss Phoenix projects confidence about her future, which in the near term includes the launch of a lingerie line. The unhappy, high school chubby duckling has indeed become the epitome of everything she was not. But the world of porn is at least as cruel as the world of high school: Search for Nikki Phoenix's body of work on any of the commercial websites that specialize in that sort of thing, and the merciless algorithms that select internet advertisements will bring up the following offer: "FUCK A FAT GIRL TONIGHT."[1]

THE LITTLE BOROUGH OF VEGAS, BABY, is practically hermetically sealed. It is surrounded by the city of Las Vegas, where hundreds of thousands of ordinary people going about their business are only vaguely aware, if they are aware at all, of the specific day-to-day operations of the industries at the core of the city's economy. The two municipalities are formally coincidental, but they are two very different places. I have dinner with some old friends who are the very picture of a happy, healthy family, the sort of enviable people who make it look easy even though it almost certainly isn't. He is a respected man in his field, she a full-time wife and mother, the two of them steady and cheerful hands on the tillers of the lives of their two engaging and energetic children, practically a Mozart duet of unwavering encouragement and gentle discipline. They hold hands around the dinner table and say grace with no sense of self-consciousness. They live in Las Vegas, but they have, as you might imagine, a complicated relationship with the borough of Vegas, Baby, plotting out driving routes that do not necessitate taking their little ones past forty-foot billboards advertising the annual porn convention.

Back when the porn industry's main concern was censorship, there was a great deal of talk about things done "in the privacy of your own home." But porn has long ago been liberated from the constraints of domestic privacy: The AVN expo is advertised by larger-than-life images of porn stars, and a towering billboard for Stripper Circus promises "The Dirtiest Show on Earth." Down at the grimy sidewalk level, the city is dotted with vending machines offering such titles as *Smut Club* and *Homo Guide*, the covers of which are more or less what the titles would lead you to expect. There are markets for everything, and this market is growing—and growing more vicious.

The libido is the engine of human history, but for the period of time we refer to as "civilization" it has been tempered and yoked. My friends' happy family is not a viable option for an increasing number of men, especially those outside of conservative religious communities. In the metropolitan areas where young men congregate, they are in almost every case outearned by the young women in the same age cohort, and under current law a marriage is far easier to walk away from than a student loan. As the French novelist Michel Houellebecq put it in his own vision of sex after humanity: "The future is female." With the institution of marriage in decay, the family in chaos, and men's traditional role as providers and protectors rendered marginal by economic reality, only the ruthless semi-simian sexual market remains, stripped naked of such traditional mediating forces as have customarily wedded male sexual energy to sociable purposes. More than that: As porn becomes less of a substitute for sexual relationships and more of an end unto itself, we are entering an era in which sex is, at least for some segment of the population, post-human. To condemn what the porn expo is offering is to miss the point: It is an inevitability. "If thine eye offend thee, pluck it out," the evangelist advises, but short of taking that radical and irreversible step, the eye is commanded, willingly or not.

We are all trenchcoats now.

Whose Streets?

Portland, Oregon

S O THERE'S THIS REALLY WHACKED-OUT YOUNG LADY just absolutely spitting high on rage with one of those weird Chelsea Girl fringe haircuts like skinhead molls used to wear back in the Age of Reagan, and she is right at this moment very fixated on—and I am not making this up—kettle corn, that weird, repulsive, caramel-coated, Dutch mutant popcorn varietal sold at state fairs and any place men in laced-up pirate blouses are gathered, and she's just going on and on about it, screaming at the top of her skinny little lungs: "It's salty and sweet! It's salty and sweet! It's salty and sweet!" and ain't nobody listening, but that's pretty clearly beside the point, psychically, from where this particular specimen is standing and chanting, working herself up into a kind of lathery confection-oriented trance as she contemplates the ineffable yin and yang of it all, kettle-corn-speaking.

I imagine that her head would explode if she found out that Oreo is making a kettle-corn-flavored sandwich cookie, and that it is—saints above!—*vegan.*

The kettle-corn girl is but one of many madcap escapees from the great mental ward of the Pacific Northwest out here making strange noises on the mean streets of downtown Portland on Election Night

2018, and her ecstatic *om mani padme hum* devotional to kettle corn is soon drowned out as her thuggish black-masked comrades begin their more straightforward and politically meaningful and considerably more comprehensible chant:

"WHOSE STREETS?"

"OUR STREETS!"

"WHOSE STREETS?"

"OUR STREETS!"

"WHOSE STREETS?"

"OUR STREETS!"

The thing is, the little pointy-headed black-shirted goons aren't wrong about that.

The official target of tonight's march is U.S. Immigration and Customs Enforcement, an agency within the Department of Homeland Security that some *Top Gun*–loving bureaucrat surely christened thus so that it could be called "ICE," which sounds about 35 percent more jackbootilicious than you really want a law-enforcement agency serving a free people in a still-functional constitutional republic to sound. "Abolish ICE!" is the official theme of the evening, and the blackshirts return to it from time to time, but the real subject of tonight's fugue is, pardon my Anglo-Saxon, "FUCK THE POLICE!" which is developed in a kind of sloppy exposition in three or four different chants.

"A-C-A-B!"

"ALL COPS ARE BASTARDS!"

"A-C-A-B!"

"ALL COPS ARE BASTARDS!"

"A-C-A-B!"

"ALL COPS ARE BASTARDS!"

And these *absolutely* are their streets, as the two neutered Portland cops following them dutifully around make clear. The goons and thugs occasionally take a moment to amuse themselves by messing with the cops, screaming obscenities at them or committing flagrant but relatively minor violations of the law in front of them, daring them to do anything about it. The cops trudge and trundle on, calm as Tibetan monks, pretending not to notice as the hoodlums pound on passing cars, block intersections, and menace bystanders. At the most public of public spaces in Portland, Pioneer Courthouse Square—"Portland's living room"—the goons encounter a little bit of counterprotest, not from sad incel Proud Boys or the Klan or from other pissant neo-fascists wearing slightly different-color shirts, but from a young black man who intuits, not inaccurately, that this is mainly a bunch of rich-white-kid playacting by little runts who make pretty good thugs when confronted with people in wheelchairs or little old ladies but who are basically chickenshit poseurs DOWN FOR THE CAUSE only to the extent that it doesn't stand between them and an oat-milk latte and an M.F.A. He says as much, at higher volume than probably is really necessary—and the weaselly little munchkin blackshirts who had just a second before insisted that ALL COPS ARE BASTARDS! and boasted of their control of the streets turn immediately to the police for help. And the police, damn their eyes, help: They evict an actual peaceable protester, if a loud one, from the public square—in order to make room for mask-wearing, law-breaking, little-old-lady-assaulting hooligans.

A police vehicle cruises down the street a respectful distance behind the mob. The purported lawmen inside announce over the loudspeakers that they are there to assure this rabble of miscreants that they are there to help the mob "exercise your First Amendment rights safely," so please stay on the sidewalk and obey the traffic laws. Naturally, the mob responds to this by immediately stepping off the sidewalk and violating the traffic laws. Not that there's any need to—they just want to remind themselves, and the police, that they can.

Whose streets? That's pretty clear.

ON *PORTLANDIA*, THE MAYOR OF PORTLAND is played by Kyle MacLachlan (of *Twin Peaks*) as a goofy and generally earnest middle-aged municipal careerist trying to be cool. In real life, Portland's mayor is Ted Wheeler, a sniveling little twerp of a bureaucrat who professes to be "appalled" at the political violence that is now commonplace on the streets of Portland but claims that he is effectively unable to do anything about it. When Antifa thugs attacked a march held by Patriot Prayer, a local right-wing group, police reported seeing people brandishing guns, clubs, knives, and pepper spray. They made no arrests.

Owing to one of the eccentricities of Portland governance, the mayor is also the police commissioner. The police chief, who bears the wonderful inaptronym "Danielle Outlaw," answers to him, as do the police themselves. According to Andy Ngo,[1] a local journalist who has written for the *Wall Street Journal* and other publications about the Portland fascists who style themselves anti-fascists, the police are under orders to avoid creating "flashpoints," meaning confrontations with hooligans that might look bad on video.

"The police are getting pushed from all sides," Ngo says. "The Right feels like the police allow anarchy to happen on the streets, and the Left says that the police are protecting the 'fascists.' The mayor's constituents are people who are sympathetic to Antifa. He's come out verbally very hard against the right-wing groups and has been inaccurate in his description of them, describing them as white supremacists, which I don't think is a fair description of Patriot Prayer or the Proud Boys. When it comes to Antifa, sometimes he condemns their violence—but never their ideology."

Mayor Wheeler did not avail himself of the opportunity to comment for this report. He did tell reporters after an earlier riot, "This is the story of Goldilocks and the two bears. The porridge is either too hot or it's too cold. At any given moment in this city, the police are criticized for being heavy-handed and intervening too quickly, or they're being criticized for being standoffish and not intervening quickly enough." Fair enough. If only Portland had some sort of city leader who in his official capacity might be relied upon to make such judgments and see them put into place through city policies. Perhaps an elected official something like what the Spanish call an *alcalde*.

The problem is most dramatically on display in Portland, but it is hardly limited to the city "where young people go to retire." Everywhere pointy-headed progressives are given unchallenged power, the same thing happens: Berkeley surrendered to political violence, too, along with Washington and other cities and practically every college campus.

Peter Beinart, writing in *The Atlantic*, forthrightly described Antifa as a group of "people preventing Republicans from safely assembling on the streets of Portland." And elsewhere, of course.

And in spite of the ridiculous rhetoric surrounding Antifa, this is very much a Democrats-versus-Republicans issue. As the blackshirts marched through Portland on the evening of the 2018 midterm elections, Democratic Party workers and campaign flunkies wearing official IDs on lanyards around their necks stepped out of the Hilton and the other places where Democratic grandees gathered to watch the returns, pumping their fists and chanting along with Antifa, sometimes looking around at one another a little guiltily. Nice, young, well-scrubbed, college-educated political professionals and volunteers cheering on a mob of masked terrorists explicitly committed to a campaign of political violence. One bloody hand washes the other.

Antifa, in Ngo's estimate, is made up of "young people who are ideologues wanting to be heroes. With the ideological monoculture in Portland, people here really think that they are in some kind of cosmic battle with fascists. So whenever there happens to be a gathering of Trump supporters—and they do it in Portland to be provocative, coming from out of town to make a point—these people, who don't have a lot of meaning in their lives, take to the streets to fight." Ngo notes that the majority of them reject religion, suggesting that they're trying to find a substitute in street violence.

"THE CRISIS OF DEMOCRACY is not a peculiarly Italian or German problem, but one confronting every modern state. Nor does it matter which symbols the enemies of human freedom choose: freedom is not less endangered if attacked in the name of anti-Fascism or in that of outright Fascism." So wrote the Freudian-Marxist social critic Erich Fromm all the way back in 1941. He knew whereof he spoke: Only a few years before, London had seen the so-called Battle of Cable Street, in which Oswald Mosley and his British Union of Fascists had attempted to march—lawfully, it is worth adding—through the city. They were attacked by thousands of anarchists, socialists, and union workers organized by the Communist Party and armed with bombs and other weapons, including bags of feces, a kind of low-rent biological weapon favored by their imitators today. They had to go through six thousand police officers, many of them mounted on horses, to get to their enemies, and they did so, crippling police horses by tossing marbles under their hooves.

Antifa has hijacked the name of an earlier German organization, Antifaschistische Aktion, a front for the Communist Party of Germany, itself a creature of Moscow and no stranger to authoritarianism, political repression, and political violence. (The Communist Party of Germany was banned in 1956 by the same constitutional court that prohibits neo-Nazi organizations.) Germany, of course, had some genuine fascists to fight, but, as in the Soviet Union itself, the term "anti-fascist" came to describe action against everything displeasing to the Kremlin. It is probably worth noting that these black-bloc hooligans do not always call themselves "Antifa." The Portland march was organized by Abolish ICE PDX. Sometimes they call themselves "Smash Racism." But they are the same people, and their goal is the same: They are fascists, albeit fascists whose idol is the proletariat rather than the nation. The helpful people at Merriam-Webster remind us that fascists seek "severe economic and social regimentation and forcible suppression of opposition." Senator Warren pursues the former, and the blackshirts pursue the latter. Their efforts are perfectly complementary. There's a reason Portland's Democratic grandees lined up to cheer on Antifa.

It is tempting to think of the street brawls between Antifa and the Proud Boys and their ilk as a kind of midget Battle of Stalingrad during which all good republicans should stand to one side and cheer for casualties. But it is more serious than that. Once political violence is out of the bottle, it is hard to put it back in. Left-wing militias such as Antifa beget right-wing militias that cite the existence of left-wing militias as justification for their own, and on and on it goes. We have seen this before in many contexts, and it rarely ends well. The original German Antifa served an enterprise whose worldwide affiliates would murder some 100 million people in the twentieth century alone.

But those were sober times. Our own are a little less so.

If you want to see what a bunch of half-baked idiots and kettle-corn psalmists in a political march are up to, the easiest thing to do is to march around with them, as I did for a while in Portland. I do not look much like Tucker Carlson, and I remain, for the moment, able to blend in with such groups.

Which I did—and a funny thing happened: As the march began to peter out, a group of Antifa loitered for a bit on a street corner, and I loitered with them for a while, observing. And then I got tired and decided to bring my labors to an end and go on my merry way. As I walked off, a contingent, apparently believing that we were once again on the move against fascism, began to follow me, pumping their fists and chanting, until they figured out that I wasn't leading them anywhere. And thus did a *National Review* correspondent end up briefly leading an Antifa march through Portland.

Of course they followed me. They'll follow anything that moves.

Sunny California, Shady Russians

The Would-Be State of Jefferson

THE IRISH REPUBLICAN PARTY and Sinn Fein still dream of a unified Irish republic. The Catalan Solidarity for Independence coalition would see the Estelada flag raised over an independent Estat Català, and there are independence-minded movements as far-flung as the western Sahara. The Uhuru Movement is a kind of separatist movement standing on its head, looking to transcend the borders of nations (with their colonial histories) and unite the African people in a single African identity. The United States has the Texas Nationalist Movement hoping to restore the Republic of Texas, and somewhere out there is a very committed fellow who believes himself to be the rightful king of Hawaii. There is a more plausible movement for an independent Puerto Rico and a much less plausible movement for an independent California. All of these have something in common.

Russians.

Weird, right?

The movement for Californian independence expects to have an initiative on the 2018 ballot, which would in turn lead to a 2019 referendum. The organizers of the "Yes California" campaign say that winning the referendum would be only the first step in the long and complex process of establishing a free and independent California, finally liberated from the grasp of Washington and the military-industrial complex. "Peace and Security" is, in fact, Exhibit A in the case for Calexit; the organizers complain that the U.S. government "spends more on its military than the next several countries combined. Not only is California forced to subsidize this massive military budget with our taxes, but Californians are sent off to fight in wars that often do more to perpetuate terrorism than to abate it. The only reason terrorists might want to attack us is because we are part of the United States and are guilty by association."

If that sounds like it could have been written by Ron Paul or some lonely disciple of Murray Rothbard, that is no accident: The leadership of the California-independence movement has a distinctly paleo smell about it.

"When I talk to people about California independence, they always say: 'Well, what would you do if China invades?'" says Yes California president Louis Marinelli from his home in . . . Yekaterinburg, formerly Sverdlovsk (city motto: DON'T CALL US SIBERIA), an industrial center on the edge of the Ural Mountains in Russia. "Seriously," he asks, "when's the last time China invaded another country?" I mention the obvious ones: Tibet, India, and the Soviet Union. There's Vietnam and Korea. Marinelli is a young man; perhaps this seems like ancient history to him. It does not to the Indians, or the Russians, or the Vietnamese. "No, I mean: When's the last time China *crossed an ocean* to invade another country?" he clarifies. "Only the United States does that."

Only?

The American war machine must surely be of some intense concern to California's would-be Jefferson Davis, inasmuch as there is no legal or constitutional process for a state's separating from the union, a question that was settled definitively, if not in court then just outside the courthouse, at Appomattox.

MARINELLI COMES FROM THE WEST COAST . . . of New York, the part of California on the shores of Lake Erie that is known as Buffalo.

He says that California is a land of immigrants, and he is proud to think of himself as one of them. He is a relatively recent arrival, having moved to San Diego in 2006, following stints in Ohio, Iowa, and Russia, where he studied in St. Petersburg and where he currently teaches English at a language institute. He believes that Californians are a culturally distinct people who simply live and think differently from the people of the other forty-nine states. It does not seem to have occurred to him that this represents only the California that exists between San Diego and San Francisco west of Interstate 5. I ask him whether he believes that people in Baker and Afton really are part of a single culture that includes the people in the Bay Area but excludes nearby Searchlight, Nevada, and Bullhead City, Arizona. He does not quite seem to know where Baker or Afton are, but speaks vaguely about "the interior." Sure, it is different, but "we're all West Coast people," he says. People from Calada, California, are West Coast people in the sense that people in Las Vegas are West Coast people, residing as they do in the Pacific Time Zone. But the folks in Calada are a lot closer to St. George, Utah, than they are to San Diego.

Perhaps we can chalk this up to the fact that Marinelli's immersion in Californian culture is fairly recent. He has been involved in politics and public affairs for some time, most prominently at the National Organization for Marriage (NOM), working against gay marriage "as if it were a disease," as he put it. After boasting of being "the one behind the 2010 Summer for Marriage Tour," he quit NOM in dramatic fashion, repudiating his previous work, apologizing for it, and publicly declaring his support for same-sex marriage, only to be mocked by *New York* magazine as a confused young man going through a "homophobic strategist for an anti-gay marriage activist organization phase." He is a Trump voter, albeit one who voted for Bernie Sanders in the Democratic primary, which he dismisses as—the inevitable word—"rigged."

"I couldn't vote for Hillary," he says. "She was the anointed candidate from the get-go. It's like we're supposed to have affirmative action in the White House now. We have to have an African-American president just because, and a woman president just because, and every demographic just because." Mrs. Clinton won nearly twice as many votes in California as Trump did. Marinelli goes on to cite the Republicans' recent failure to repeal the Affordable Care Act and "gridlock" in Washington as evidence that California would be better governed by Californians. California is, in fact, one of the states where residents on balance think themselves better off with the Affordable Care Act than without it, according to a Hoover Institution poll. Which is to say, the leader of the California-independence movement is politically at odds, deeply so, with the great majority of Californians.

On the upside, the great majority of Californians haven't heard of him.

"I SUPPOSE IT HAS A CERTAIN ROMANTIC APPEAL," says Judith Montgomery, a Bay Area math teacher who, like many Californians, is aware that there is a vote coming on a quixotic independence campaign but finds the notion impossible to take seriously. She mentions *Ecotopia*, Ernest Callenbach's influential 1975 novel about a different version of California secession, one in which the state joins with Oregon and Washington to form a new "stable-state" nation based on environmental principles, which in 1975 apparently included Bhutanese-style isolation and autarky—the novel's premise is that the green utopia is receiving its first American visitor in twenty years. "*Ecotopia* was my favorite book when I was twenty-one," she says. "I'm in my sixties now, and the world doesn't work like that."

The secession talk, she says, is a waste of time and—more objectionable, in her view—a waste of money that might be better used elsewhere. She insists that she's "not the best-informed person," but her concerns are the concerns of people who are paying attention to, for example, California's grossly wasteful duplication of administrative jobs in education, something Governor Arnold Schwarzenegger promised to address but failed to deliver on. That's the stuff of which actual governance is made, and it isn't very exciting.

Redrawing the map is exciting. It is so exciting that Yes California not only isn't the only secessionist movement underway in the United

States, it isn't even the only active campaign to redraw the map in California. Former UK Independence party leader Nigel Farage, of all people, is involved in a project to split the state into a Western and Eastern California, liberating the more conservative and agrarian half of the state from the half of the state where the money and the people are. And there is the long-standing dream of the State of Jefferson, which would strip away several of California's northernmost counties (the proposed capital is Yreka) and some of southern Oregon's to form a new state—one with a very high regard for the Tenth Amendment.

They hotly dispute any comparison to Yes California—"We want to add a star to the flag, not take one away!" insists Jefferson supporter Terry Rapoza—but at bottom there is a set of commonalities: the sense that the ordinary democratic institutions as currently configured are insufficient for the times; the feeling that some people are effectively unrepresented, a relatively small group of broadly like-minded people who form only a few drops in the vast sea of American democracy; the belief that radical action oriented toward separation is required. "I don't want to do this," says Rapoza. "Show me a way not to do this." He is in regular touch with his state senator and other California elected officials, and he says his message for them is: "Help us to help you help us."

But Rapoza is pessimistic about the chances of California's Democratic majority—"the monoparty," he calls it—getting serious about things like the rule of law and fiscal responsibility. He recites the familiar litany: high taxes and fees that contrast dramatically with crumbling roads and infrastructure—the Oroville Dam emergency seems to have opened a great many eyes—poor schools, unfunded pension liabilities, crime, and sanctuary cities that encourage illegal immigration. "We have one senator. Los Angeles has eleven. Who wins that football game?" Rapoza asks. He takes a moment to reconsider the metaphor. "Maybe if you had Tom Brady."

LIKE THE LEADERSHIP OF YES CALIFORNIA, the counties that would form the State of Jefferson went overwhelmingly for Trump. Mrs.

Clinton pounded Trump in California and reduced him nearly to third-party numbers in places such as San Francisco, but Trump outperformed her in the Jefferson counties by a larger margin than the one she enjoyed in California as a whole. The Jefferson activists are old-fashioned patriots who sound like Tea Party guys: Tenth Amendment, high taxes, too much debt, too much regulation, too much welfare spending on too many illegal immigrants. Yes California's Louis Marinelli has a pretty right-wing outlook and history, albeit one that is more Robert A. Taft than Ronald Reagan. What's funny is that his Calexit campaign wasn't doing very much until something happened that almost nobody in California was expecting. Marinelli cast a protest vote for Donald Trump, but the guy turned around and won.

Suddenly, secession started to sound more promising not to paleo-libertarian Californians hiding out in Big Sur cabins but to ordinary, progressive, Democratic-voting Californians of the familiar variety. Shervin Pishevar, a big-money tech investor with a hand in everything from Uber to Hyperloop, declared himself a California separatist after Trump was elected and said he was "funding a legitimate campaign for California to become its own nation." Other Silicon Valley figures, such as venture capitalist Jason Calacanis, joined in. And Marinelli's phone started ringing.

"We have thousands of people literally waiting for us to even get the opportunity to contact them by phone," Marinelli says. "There are sixty chapters, and each has a chapter leader. We have eight thousand registered volunteers." He says he received more than seventeen thousand emails in November and December following the election. "Some of them are hate mail, but a lot are people who want to help."

He is getting some help—from the Anti-Globalization Movement of Russia, which is, depending on whom you ask, either a group that enjoys some financial backing from the Kremlin or an outright Kremlin front. It provides Marinelli with office space in Moscow, where he has opened a kind of California embassy, a cultural center whose most recent exhibition was on civil rights. (Short version: California good, United States bad.) It provided travel expenses for those far-flung separatists from around the world to attend the conference it organized in Moscow, although the king of Hawaii was unable to attend in person and sent video greetings. Marinelli says he supports the Texas Nationalist Movement and others who attended the event in Moscow. And he scoffs at the notion that the Kremlin might be attempting to use him and his daft little crusade for its own ends. "Meddling in other countries' elections is the sort of thing the United States does," he says. His anti-Americanism is deep and it is reflexive. He says it would be "hypocrisy" for Americans to complain about Moscow's meddling in the internal affairs of other countries. I ask him to consider that even if it were hypocritical, that would not make it untrue. He responds as subtly as people who believe as he believes always respond. "The United States supported the Taliban."

His Russian friends and allies share his belief that the United States should not be in a position of "dominating the world," he says, and he adds that they share his belief in the self-determination of peoples. That would come as news to, among many others, Rafis Kashapov, a Tatar dissident imprisoned for criticizing Moscow's annexation of Crimea. He was found guilty of *advocating separatism*—which of course is illegal in Russia. He did not join Marinelli and the others at the Moscow Ritz-Carlton.

The Russian oligarchs are awash with money and in thrall to a kind of atavistic nationalism, and they have a lot of cash to throw around at things like separatist movements in California or Spain or Ireland or any other place they think they might wrong-foot the West, however slightly. And where the West comes to an end on the sunny beaches of the Pacific, they have an ally. At least when he's visiting from the edge of Siberia.

Der Apfelstrudelführers

Dallas

"WINDOW NINJA, WHAT'S YOUR TWENTY?"
          The militia is here, in the park next to city hall, on patrol,
pretty decently armed up with 7.62×39mm rifles, pudgy faces concealed
behind olive drab keffiyehs, radios crackling with status reports, eyes
presumably alert behind the polarized aviators they're not quite ready to
give up in spite of the weak light of the early dusk, and they are ready—
and, by God, eager!—to stand tall in Texas and enforce justice for the
law, an eagerness that is kind of hilarious even if it is something a lot less
than amusing to the actual law-enforcement officers here, standing stiff-
necked and rigid behind steel-tube barricades with their riot batons and
helmets casually arranged on the thick August summer grass behind
them, watching as the setting sun sends the long shadow of Robert E.
Lee falling across the various and sundry wackos, prodigal sons of the
Confederacy, sad little left-wing collegiate tomboys playing radical dress-
up with red bandanas over their faces like spaghetti-western bandits and
SMASH THE FASH! placards, conspiracy theorists who want you to know
what the Federal Reserve—the creature from Jekyll Island!—is really up
to, old-fashioned rednecks whose T-shirts proclaim them Stone Cold
Country by the Grace of God, weird skinny twitchy guys who mention

in every other sentence that they served in the Marines and who probably didn't actually serve in the Marines, self-described free speech activists, that inevitable dude with the mullet waving the Confederate flag, guys in homemade riot gear slapped together from dusty hunting and motor-cycling equipment, acres of sad dreary desert-camo cargo pants over coyote-tan boots from the Army surplus shop, Communists, anarchists, extravagant beards, TV cameras, dreadlocks, ponytails, banana maga-zines protruding from matte-black Kalashnikov knockoffs, cases of bottled water provided by the City of Dallas for your dissident conve-nience, Antifa and Antifa wannabes, Democratic Party organizers, cotton-candy vendors, at least three kinds of police, including Dallas mounties on big fine gray horses, the whole mess kind of milling about counterclockwise, a slow-motion hurricane of human angst and rage and boredom and more rage.

A couple of hundred people are here at the side protest in a largely Confederate cemetery, trampling on the graves of Civil War veterans and widows and on group graves for young children felled by the many ter-rors of the nineteenth century. The main show, with the speeches and sound system and all, is across the way at city hall.

Somewhere in the shadows, Window Ninja is watching. A silent sentinel, a watcher in the dusk.

At the eye of the hurricane, at least for a minute, is the local ambas-sador from the Republic of Kekistan.

Maybe you don't know about Kekistan, which was Boogaloo before Boogaloo was. Here's the deal, from the website Know Your Meme: "The Cult of Kek, also known as the Church of Kek, is a satirical religion based around the worship of the ancient Egyptian deity Kek (also spelled Kuk or Keku), an androgynous God of darkness and chaos who is often depicted as a frog or frog-headed man in male form or a snake-headed woman in female form. On 4chan, the character Pepe the Frog is often considered a modern avatar of the diety [sic], who uses ancient Egyptian meme magic to influence the world, often by fulfilling the wishes of posts that end in repeating numbers."

Kek is another silly in-joke from the Dumb Green Frog Gang, the internet *apfelstrudelführers* of the so-called alt-right, and it's a pretty good example of their *modus dumbasseri*. The flag of Kekistan is a Nazi battle flag with the blood scarlet replaced by Pepe green and the swastika at the center transformed into a Kek cross, four "K"s arranged around a central "E." When three "K"s aren't enough . . .

"It's a parody!" screams the slightly porky man from Kekistan, who has literally wrapped himself in the flag, wearing it like a superhero's cape. The crowd isn't having any of it. "It's based on a Nazi flag!" comes the response from the skinny little kid in the yarmulke. "That's . . . *not OK!*" The crowd moves in on the Kekistani, who insists that he isn't a racist or a neo-Nazi or anything like that—in fact, he says, he doesn't even particularly care about the Confederate statues here in the park adjacent to city hall, which, in theory, is what this pageant of rage is really all about—he is, he says, simply here to exercise his free speech. Free speech about what? He either doesn't know or won't say.

"I'm not a Nazi!"

The girls in the red bandanas creep in, eyes wide, ready to SMASH THE FASH! as hard as their soft pink little fists can smash. He's sweating and squealing and wide-eyed and pretty clearly thinking about when he read *Lord of the Flies* in high school as the crowd tightens in around him, the eye of the rage hurricane contracting on his person. But nothing happens. It's like kids at a junior-high dance: Somebody has to make the first move, otherwise the boys and the girls just stay on their own respective sides of the gym and never start dancing. The bandana brigades came for a riot, but they will go home disappointed.

Slick takes it all in. Slick has traveled to this protest from . . . somewhere . . . and he doesn't want to be interviewed or to give his name. Amid the various kooks and cranks and goons and mall-ninja militiamen, he's a slick little fucker indeed, neat church-boy haircut, buttondown shirt, khakis, pristine Nikes. No fatigues and swastikas and Confederate flags for him. He's like a miniature Richard Spencer, twenty years younger and still enjoying his anonymity. Aloof and ironic, he's an organizer, on the phone at intervals with somebody somewhere, making his report.

"The mayor of Charlottesville is a Democrat," he explains, "and a Jew."

This gets the attention of the little gaggle of protesters who had spent the better part of an hour standing around a Confederate flag and swapping cigarettes and conspiracy theories—fluoridation and the other classics—among themselves before Slick showed up on the scene. "So, he wanted chaos, and he got it. He wanted all the havoc he could. And people died." He tells an exculpatory version of the Charlottesville story in which the police, not the white nationalists, are at fault: The "free-speech activists," who were chanting about Jews and flying swastika banners, were a peaceful bunch, he says, not looking for any trouble, and, rather than do the usual thing and keep the police between the "free-speech activists" with the Nazi regalia and the Antifa thugs looking to SMASH THE FASH!, the Charlottesville police plotted to push them together in order to provoke violence that could be blamed on the boys from Kekistan.

Someone lays a hand on the Kekistani's chest: "Do not touch me!" he screams, and what ensues is a little game of "I'm Not Touching You!" that will be familiar to anybody who ever spent much time in the back of a station wagon on a long family road trip.

The cotton-candy guy does steady business. A fair profit, nothing more.

A guy shooting video on his iPhone interviews one of the militiamen, and he's going on and on about the militiaman's rifle and its ammunition: "Full metal jacket!" he repeats, over and over, apparently unaware that jacketed ammunition has been the standard for some time—since 1899, in fact. A young black woman on a cheerful pink bicycle rides past and pauses to take in the show. The dramatic contrast is of interest to the guy shooting the video, and he points it out to the militiaman. "You're here with your rifle, with your full-metal-jacket ammunition, and here's this *little girl* on her bicycle." She leans in to speak to him. "Here's this thirty-year-old woman on her bicycle," he corrects himself.

Slick puts on his red Make America Great Again cap and wades into the scrum.

"CONVENTIONAL REPUBLICANS" is how he describes his parents, chuckling. "Episcopalians," he adds with a little snort.

"I had a very normal childhood in Dallas," says Richard Spencer, the slickest and most notorious racist in American public life since David Duke. "I went to St. Mark's"—that's a $28,000-a-year prep school—"and I was on the football team. But I was interested in some more avant-garde things." He directed and starred in a school performance of *K2*, Patrick Meyers's 1983 Broadway play about a doomed mountaineering expedition. "It's a real . . . *masculine* play," Spencer says, with just a hint of self-derision in his soft voice. "It's about two mountain climbers climbing K2. One leaves the other to die. Very Nietzschean." His interest in theater continued into his adulthood. "At UVA, I directed my own productions, including a very avant-garde, Robert Wilson–like version of *Hamlet*. I was looking for something beyond pedestrian reality and bourgeois society."

Richard Spencer isn't a storm trooper. He's a theater kid.

The nexus of fascism and the avant-garde is familiar territory, from the Italian Futurists to Le Corbusier. Poor rotten old syphilitic Freddy Nietzsche provides the shared philosophical basis, or at least the shared intellectual *posture*: The new man and the new civilization must be pulled forth out of the corruption and decadence of the present by intellectual and/or physical violence. If a white nationalist's name-checking a gay experimental-theater icon sounds weird to you, you aren't paying close enough attention. The so-called alt-right is not about politics: It is about aesthetics. And though it shares some political space with conservatism and, thanks to Donald Trump, with the Republican Party, the alt-right isn't exactly right, either: Richard Spencer is a pro-choice atheist with some substantial reservations about capitalism, a man who mocks the Republicans as a bunch of Babbitts who cannot see that life contains "more than free trade and tax cuts." And he is, inescapably, a deep-dyed

Nietzschean. Or at least he thinks he is, and he describes his first encounter with *The Genealogy of Morals* as "a shattering experience." He is insistent in his belief that people do not really change over time, a point to which he returns several times. Reading Nietzsche is as close to a transformative experience as he'll allow.

Transformation is a theme in his life. He talks about having lost a lot of weight after "bulking up" to play offensive tackle in high school, and he is famously vain about his looks. He affects a "fashy" razor haircut with a little lock arranged to casually fall just so over his right eye and often dresses in pastoral tweeds like he's hunting grouse on an English country manor. He is much more interested in the aesthetics of his movement than he is in any specific policy ideas, a subject about which he is in fact quite vague. "I recognize the power of spectacle," he says. "It could even be something as simple as looking good—something conservatives could learn from. Politics isn't just about dusty ideas or arcane policy matters. The question isn't whether you're about politics or about theatrics, because those aren't different things. But is it just theatrics? Speaking for me, absolutely not." Asked for his top three policy-agenda items, he gets no further than numbers one and two: a net-zero immigration policy and "a tremendous change in foreign policy." He says the usual thing about "neoconservatives" hoping to bomb the world into democracy.

He likes Depeche Mode and "peaceful" ethnic cleansing and rejects the label "white supremacist," and he is obviously and painfully embarrassed by the swastika flags and silly costumes that invariably show up in the crowds he attracts, though he has been known to throw out a Heil or two himself—he'll cop to having been "trollish" on occasion—as he did when celebrating the election of Donald Trump, the alt-right hero whose shine has quickly worn off, at least for America's most infamous white nationalist. "Swastikas are not my style. But once you declare, 'I am a white American, I am proud of my heritage, my identity matters, I am not just an individual, not just interested in free markets and tax cuts,' then you get the 'H' word or the 'N' word. People get called 'Nazi,' and they want to throw it back in the face of their adversary. And some people are stuck in the past, and they're not able to understand that we need to live here and now, and not in the 1920s or the 1940s. Others *want* to alienate themselves from society. My strategy is to be provocative and radical in the best sense, but also to communicate with"—here is a favored bit of alt-right lingo—"the normies."

Spencer's career traces the arc of the alt-right's intellectual development. He thought of himself as part of the Right, broadly attached to the conservative movement, in spite of his secularism and his distaste for religion and religiously informed politics. He studied at Virginia, did a master's in humanities at the University of Chicago, and worked at the *American Conservative*, the right-wing periodical co-founded by Pat Buchanan. When his views proved too extreme for that journal, he moved on to Taki's Magazine. He founded a website of his own and soon occupied a number of high positions in the relatively tiny world of white-nationalist intellectual life: executive director of the race-obsessed Washington Summit Publishers, founder of the white-nationalist journal Radix, and director of the National Policy Institute, a racist think tank supported by William Regnery II. Playing a game of Six Degrees of Separation between mainstream conservative institutions and white-nationalist nuttery is an uncomfortable exercise for many on the right. There's a great deal of political and intellectual space between a traditionalist Christian conservative such as Rod Dreher of the *American Conservative* and a guy waving a swastika flag and raving about "white genocide," and Richard Spencer inhabits some of that space, with a foot and a history in both camps. He is frank—more than frank—about his white-identity politics, but he does not so much as mention Jews, blacks, or any other traditional target of fringe-right hatred. "What's misunderstood is that people think our movement is about hate, that it can be equated with past movements and cartoon versions of past movements, with Nazis and the Klan foaming at the mouth about hatred. I would not do what I do if I were dominated by hate. Hate is an emotion we all feel. I hate *injustice*. But what is truly motivating is hope: a vision of a better, more beautiful world." What's important for Spencer isn't winning elections or changing public policy but changing the culture, developing a new and publicly acceptable ethic in which "white people think of themselves as part of a greater story and broader community." He went on Israeli television and described himself as a Zionist for white Americans.

What Spencer gets—and exploits—is the American sensitivity to unfairness, real or perceived. That deeply rooted sense of justice as fairness, combined with the American tendency to universalize principles, explains why, for example, gay rights groups have been so successful in adopting the rhetoric of the African-American civil rights movement. The American fairness ethic is basically a good-for-the-goose-good-for-the-gander-ism. And so Spencer, and others like him, ask: If blacks are permitted pride in themselves as black people, and if we accept a collectively self-interested black politics as legitimate, why are whites not permitted pride in themselves as white people, and why is a collectively self-interested white politics not also legitimate? Spencer says that it is inaccurate to describe him as a "white supremacist" in that he has no interest in seeing whites dominate other races. What he wants, he says, is a "safe space." If the Jews can have a physically secure ethno-religious state, Spencer asks, then why not white Americans, including "cultural Christians" like him?

Highlighting these perceived hypocrisies and acts of unfairness is what the style adopted by Spencer and the rest of the alt-right—he coined the term "alt-right"—is intended to do. It is all but impossible to argue someone out of a perception, and the "mimetic warfare" of the alt-right, all that internet ugliness and trollery, is designed to change perceptions. It appeals to the adolescent appetite for transgression, the *épater les bourgeois* ethic of radical youth movements around the world. A generation ago, when Sid Vicious of the Sex Pistols performed wearing a swastika T-shirt, no one thought it was because punk rock was anti-Semitic or that the Sex Pistols hated Jews. It was shocking for the sake of being shocking. That is the shelter into which the alt-right retreats when it is challenged—the Kekistani guy at the city hall protest shouting "It's a parody!" while wearing his Nazi-inspired flag. But the act of being shocking, as the Sex Pistols' accountants could tell you, is effective. The Sieg Heil stuff may be done partly, though not entirely, tongue in cheek, but the next part of the pitch—"Let me tell you why the white-nationalist movement is like Zionism"—is deadly serious. It's a performance, but a performance with a purpose.

In other words: "Let's put on a show!" And there's no business like show business, until somebody gets killed.

HEAR, OH HEAR, THIS TALE OF WOE, this poetical lament:

Many of us have student loans on degrees that are worthless.
    Many of us fought in wars for Jews.
    Many of us have struggled with substance abuse.
    Many of us are out of shape.
    We feel emasculated.
    Many of us feel we have never had power.
    We crave power.
    We lust after power. We want to be part of a group, which will give us power. A group that will confirm our worth as men.
    We do not have identities.
    We want identities.
    We want to be productive. All men want to be productive. We want to build things. We want to build, we want to create, we want to be needed.
    We have problems with women. All of us do. We lie to each other and claim that we don't.
    We are a generation of throwaways, which (((those who write history before it happens))) have slated to be the last generation
    of Heterosexual White Men.
    We are angry.

There is an atavistic rage in us, deep in us, that is ready to
boil over.

There is a craving to return to an age of violence.

We want a war.

Andrew Anglin is the founder of the Daily Stormer, a now-defunct
neo-Nazi website that served as a clearinghouse for alt-right white
nationalism and also as a bellwether for its aesthetic. The above complaint, written for some reason as though it were lines of verse, is his
confession, his *apologia pro* sad little *vita sua*. The Daily Stormer has
been disappeared from the internet by the Corporate Powers That Be,
but Anglin is still moping around.

Anglin is more frank about the Nazi stuff than Spencer is; he once
wrote that he asks himself "WWHD"—"What Would Hitler Do?"
But get what he means by that: "I ask myself what Hitler would do
if he'd been born in 1984 in America and was dealing with this situation we are currently dealing with and also really liked 4chan and
anime," he writes. Anglin, like Spencer, says that he thinks it is
important for the alt-right to forgo the old style of "White Nationalism 1.0," as he puts it, and try to be, in his word, "cool." But what
you really find in Anglin is the cultural intersection that is the home
to the alt-right, the nexus between the transgressive and provocative
politics of white identity and the saddest and uncoolest and cringiest
of all American social movements: the men's movement. It's easy to
make jokes about how all this fringy rage is just the natural outcome
of a bunch of 4chan geeks who couldn't get laid in a sex-doll factory,
but their own rhetoric and discourse continually returns to that
theme. It is an ancient story: The sons of the effete white ruling class
feel emasculated in comparison to the swarthy high-testosterone
primitives from . . . that part gets kind of interesting, inasmuch as
there was a time when the American WASP felt sexually intimidated
by Asians, Jews, and Italians, though it is the mythic sexual rapacity
of the African that has most kept them up at night.

Muppet News Flash: A bunch of underemployed anime nerds marching with tiki torches in rage-fueled sausage fests turn out to be guys who have trouble with women.

After the protest in Charlottesville—in which a woman was murdered by a white nationalist—Anglin advised his fellow knuckleheads to go out to bars that night, because "random girls will want to have sex with you." One wonders whether Charlottesville is home to very many women who are quite that random. The men's movement has moved on from *Iron John* and suburbanite drum circles and virile weeping and all that business, and its new spokesmen are the pickup artists, whose appeal to men (put an asterisk there) such as Andrew Anglin is pretty obvious. Like Islamic jihadists promised an eternity with a harem of virgins, white-identity jihadists believe that they can elevate themselves through conflict and confrontation and, by proving their value to the tribe, finally get some nookie.

"We want a war," writes Anglin.

He is barely five feet tall.

BUT EVERYBODY IS TEN FEET TALL ON THE INTERNET, and that is why the internet is where the alt-right really lives, one big online group-therapy session masquerading as a political movement. A few sad specimens will occasionally sally forth into the public square in Charlottesville, Boston, or Dallas, and there will always be an opening for a charismatic racist such as Richard Spencer, who holds a position in American life that once belonged to David Duke, and to George Lincoln Rockwell before him. Some roles in our common life are passed down from generation to generation. And some kinds of sadness are passed down from generation to generation, too: the substance abuse that Anglin bemoans tends to run in families, as does divorce—and the failure to form marriages and families in the first place. The young men to whom Anglin addresses his lament are themselves often the sons and grandsons of similarly disappointed men, living in communities left behind by globalization and other social changes, from which anyone with the wherewithal to move on is already long gone.

Without prestigious jobs, solid incomes, or happy families to provide them with social status or meaning to their lives, they understand themselves to be failures not only as people but specifically as men. In reaction to the "rootless cosmopolitanism" of the age, they seek to reverse twenty-first-century deracination with blood-and-soil *racination*: Consider that Richard Spencer's journal is called Radix, that is, "root." Their longing for community is authentic—and it is legitimate, in spite of the horrifying direction in which they take it. But like all men who are missing something necessary at the center of them, they are born to be marks, and it is easy to sell them almost anything—how-to-meet-women books and seminars, conspiracy theories, daft white-identity politics—so long as what you are really selling is hope.

Down and Out in R.A.T.T. Town

Camp R.A.T.T., Texas

I N THE 1990S, WHEN THE GREAT MILLENNIAL TECH BOOM was really
just getting going and the sudden presence of fresh shiny silver and
black Volkswagen Jettas announced the arrival of an unexpected new
kind of energetic high-momentum young money on the streets of Austin—formerly a sleepy college town famous for the stylishly unambitious
young white people captured with anthropological precision in Richard
Linklater's *Slacker*—Interstate 35 formed the great imposing socioeconomic Berlin Wall between the high-on-irony undergraduate Caucasians
eating spinach enchiladas and taking seven years to get a bachelor's
degree over at the University of Texas and the earnestly and unironically
poor and brown and dangerous precincts of East Austin. Big Tech money
changed all that, and by the end of the 1990s Austin had a higher apart-
ment-occupancy rate than New York City's. Students looking for rentals
would go around with their brokers and their checkbooks (or their
parents' checkbooks) ready to sign a lease on the spot as soon as they
found a half-decent place they could afford, while the young graduates
working at Dell and AMD had oodles of new money to spend. Suddenly,
all that sprawling East Austin real estate adjacent to the university and
downtown became much more attractive, and the city's residential

developers and realtors and hipsters and slackers all did the Berlin Wall thing in reverse, crossing the border from west to east, following a small vanguard of college students and artists who preceded them in search of low rents and joblessness opportunities.

But the Jetta people, too, grew more and more wealthy and discriminating and finicky, and East Austin is now a whole 'nother thing entirely, a sunny warm little Brooklyn of vegan restaurants and yoga studios and fashionable craft-cocktail bars, with a clubhouse for the runners who work at Favor and a bunch of those weird cool-kid retail establishments with names like "Jacoby's Mercantile." There's a short line out the door on Saturday morning for an establishment offering "plant-based meals" and an understandably longer one—thirty deep at least—outside la Barbecue, which sells $15 Frito-pie sandwiches ("pulled pork, chopped beef, chipotle slaw, beans, Fritos, cheese and jalapeños, served on a Martin potato bun") and brisket at $22.95 a pound.

There's another line down the street as the residents of a homeless camp on Cesar Chavez Boulevard line up for their Saturday morning visit from Mobile Loaves & Fishes, a joint ministry of several downtown churches and volunteers that sends trucks into Austin's streets 365 days a year with food, clothing, and other supplies. The scene is as bleak and ugly and oh-the-humanity as you'd expect, but there isn't any evidence of the piles of feces and used heroin needles that Texas governor Greg Abbott described in his October ultimatum to Austin mayor Steve Adler, demanding that the city "demonstrate consequential improvement in the Austin homelessness crisis" by November 1 or expect intervention from the state government. There's a "No Solicitation Area" sign nearby, a reminder of East Austin's previous incarnation as a zone of infamy with street-corner drug dealers and open prostitution, but the encampment itself is quiet enough. (The neighborhood is, at least on this Saturday morning, heavily policed.) And while it is not exactly what you'd call spick-and-span, it isn't the stuff of talk-radio horror stories, either. What it is, really, is simply out of place, a little island of filth and despair and old-fashioned human agony in the midst of all that carefully subtle hipster consumerism.

CONSERVATIVES USED TO JOKE BITTERLY that homelessness is a problem in America only when there's a Republican president—or that's what you'd think, they said, if you knew the world only through the pages of the *New York Times*. The political tables have turned, with conservatives pointing to homelessness in cities from Washington to Los Angeles and San Francisco as the reification of despair in Democratic-run cities.

Austin, a lost city as far as Republicans are concerned, has become Texas's rhetorical whipping boy for homelessness and urban untidiness in part because it is a famously smug and insufferable citadel of Molly Ivins–style progressivism in the state that has been stereotyped as the heart of belligerent Trump-style Republicanism, making the capital city a culturally attractive target for Governor Abbott and other like-minded conservatives even though the situation here is not much different from what one sees in other Texas cities. A spokesman for Governor Abbott disputes that and maintains that the situation in Austin is dramatically different from that of, say, Houston or San Antonio. "We are not going to let Austin become another San Francisco," he says. However Austin compares with the other big cities in Texas, it is worth keeping in mind that those cities are no less dominated by Democrats than Austin is.

Texas is, as everybody knows, a solidly Republican state, except for Austin . . . and Houston, San Antonio, Dallas, El Paso, and practically every other city of any consequence: Ted Cruz lost Fort Worth to Robert Francis O'Rourke in 2018, leaving Lubbock as the largest reliably Republican-voting city in the state. Texas is in many ways a New Deal state, one that was until the 1990s mostly run by relatively conservative Democrats (Rick Perry dutifully flacked for Al Gore's presidential campaign in 1988 before switching parties, though it is a fiction that he was Gore's Texas chairman) and capable of electing a genuine progressive such as Ann Richards to its highest office. The new terror over homelessness is at least in part a Republican political indictment of cities per se and of urban political and cultural habits—which are the major long-term threat to Republican power in Texas and nationally.

Donald Trump won only 35 percent of the vote in Dallas County and 26 percent in El Paso County. (He scored down in the *teens* in border counties such as Starr, worse than he did in Austin.) Houston hasn't seen a Republican mayor since the 1980s. Julián Castro is at least as typical of Texas politics as Ted Cruz is. Austin and every other big city in Texas have big-city politics and big-city problems.

Senator Cruz may not be all that popular nationwide, but Austin sure as hell is. The local builders can't build fast enough to keep up with demand: Austin has led the country in population growth every year for almost a decade—6.7 percent of the people living in Austin in 2018 lived somewhere else in 2017. Overall, the population has grown by more than 20 percent in just eight years. Unlike much of the rest of Texas, Austin is a relatively difficult place for middle-income people. Like San Francisco and similar cities, Austin is run by nice rich white liberals who grow richer and whiter by the day. Median household income, already well above the national average, is growing at 6.6 percent annually.

In 1990, African Americans made up 12.4 percent of Austin's population. Today, they make up less than 8 percent of its residents—but 42 percent of its homeless.

In reality, neither Austin nor Texas is quite what outsiders think: Austin's politics is a progressivism of pronouns and greenwashed NIMBYism, a blend of campus-radical posturing and NPR-listening lifestyle liberalism that is a good deal less politically serious than the traditional city-machine politics and aggressive anti-capitalism that characterizes left-wing politics in larger Texas cities such as Houston and San Antonio.

As local groups providing services to the homeless run the numbers, Austin has *less* homelessness relative to its population than do similar cities such as Denver and Seattle. Austin counts about 2,200 homeless out of a population of just under 1 million; San Francisco, with a population of 884,000, counts more than 8,000 homeless.

But while the severity of Austin's problem may be exaggerated, those homeless camps are a real thing. Republicans aren't making them up.

You see them in quickly developing neighborhoods such as the area surrounding the intersection of State Highway 183 and Burnet Road, where a young woman in a black sports bra and cargo pants the color of sadness goes wheeling and staggering madly through traffic outside an encampment of tents and carefully locked-up bicycles under the overpass. Nearby, seedy-looking CBD shops and massage parlors do business.

Mainly, though, the homeless are being pushed out of the shiniest parts of town into places such as Montopolis, a nineteenth-century village on the site of a former freedmen's community that eventually was absorbed into East Austin and populated largely by low-income black and Latino residents. "One could trace, like rings in a tree, the modern history of Montopolis by the types of affordable housing built in each decade," Michael Barnes wrote in a 2016 essay in the *Austin American-Statesman*. The nearby Bastrop Highway, which is currently undergoing a major expansion, looks set to become the city's new Berlin Wall of money and college credentials. Take a right at the intersection with Montopolis Drive, which runs through the heart of the old community, and you'll arrive at a roadside sign discreetly announcing Camp R.A.T.T.

"I'M A WEEKEND MOM, NOW," SAYS T-BOOG. She's building a firepit in front of her tent for cooking and warmth, assembling stray bricks and fragments of cinder block. Her daughter, who is listening to music on the stereo of a car parked nearby, turns the music down and turns her face away. T-Boog has been living here at Camp R.A.T.T.—"Responsible Adult Transition Town"—for a few weeks. It is a new facility, though "facility" is probably not quite the right word. As the political volleys between Governor Abbott and Mayor Adler went back and forth, with the city resolving and then unresolving to enforce its "urban camping" ordinance—as though this were about camping—the inevitable question came up: If Austin clears out the homeless camps, then where do the homeless go? The answer the state came up with is five acres of blasted dusty state-owned land near Montopolis Drive, walled and gated and concertina-wired and overseen by two smiling and friendly agents from the state's Division of Emergency Management, who normally are tasked with managing the aftereffects of hurricanes and tornadoes rather than the slow-motion man-made disaster whose effects are being funneled here into Camp R.A.T.T., which the residents originally had called "Camp Abbott" before settling on the more aspirational name they've given their community.

This is not T-Boog's first experience with tent life. Before, she lived in an encampment "in the woods," she says. A couple of large settlements have been discovered over the years in Austin's greenbelt. Camp R.A.T.T. gives its residents some respite that they do not enjoy elsewhere. They are living here with the state's begrudging consent, so they do not have to worry about being chased away from whatever semi-permanent arrangements they can make, and there are daily deliveries of water and food in the form of MREs. Like all of the Camp R.A.T.T. residents I speak to, T-Boog is not an Austin native. She comes most recently from Orlando but prefers the less swampy climate here. One of her neighbors comes from San Diego but has in recent years traveled all over the country, from California to the Carolinas. T-Boog says she has a hard time keeping a job because she always wants to try new things. She applied for an online degree program in "entrepreneurship" but was unable to enroll because she doesn't have regular access to an internet connection. Things went bad for her after a divorce. Her daughter comes to visit her on the weekends, but she doesn't let her stay overnight. "It's not safe," she says.

T-Boog is a classic kind of American delusional. "Socialism never took root in America because the poor see themselves not as an exploited proletariat but as temporarily embarrassed millionaires," Ronald Wright wrote in his *History of Progress*. T-Boog is living in a tent but imagines reinventing herself as a serial entrepreneur. Another resident speaks of his plans to do something "with media."

There are obvious downsides to tent life, T-Boog says, but there are parts of it she likes, too. "I like the self-sufficiency," she explains. "Like building this firepit. I like doing things myself." It's a funny kind of "self-sufficiency," of course, with daily rations delivered by the state, but

T-Boog insists that in Camp R.A.T.T. she is "free" in a way that she can't be "out there."

And maybe she is.

The people in Camp R.A.T.T. have put forward a few community leaders to represent them and their interests, though their agenda remains, for the moment, pretty vague. They have organized a committee to canvass for donations and another to organize work details in the camp. The state agents say they do not know anything about this, being aware only that the organization effort exists. "That's something they came up with themselves," one says.

Among the residents of Camp R.A.T.T., there is a great deal of the painfully familiar passive language (and passive thinking) characteristic of the American underclass: One Camp R.A.T.T. resident speaks of losing his previous rental arrangement after "the altercation . . . that *occurred*," as though he had been only a spectator. And there also is a great deal of the sudden veering turns into crackpottery typical of conversation with people who are suffering from untreated mental illness. Barry, an older man living at Camp R.A.T.T. who is hopeful that he will soon transition into a stable housing arrangement, is friendly and calm when telling his story, and then casually remarks that U.S. cities have gone into "lockdown" because of "something happening in Iraq."

Matt Mollica, the director of ECHO, a nonprofit that works with the homeless, contests the widely held view that homelessness is mainly a mental health and addiction issue. Of course homelessness and mental illness overlap, he says, but homelessness is itself something like an addiction in the sense that certain people are "predisposed to it, like being predisposed to a medical condition." Bearing in mind all of the usual caveats that apply to self-reported data, we might say that homeless people in Austin are much more likely to report a physical disability keeping them from work than mental-health or substance-abuse problems. At the same time, there are millions of people who lose their jobs, experience mental-health problems, become disabled, or get thrown out of their apartments without becoming homeless. Some people bounce back; some people fall and can't get up. The overwhelming majority of people who are homeless in Austin would prefer to be in regular housing of some kind, but they cannot quite get there.

"FOLKS DON'T UNDERSTAND HOMELESSNESS," Mollica says. "It's hard for them to put themselves in that experience."

Properly understood, what the hundred-plus residents of Camp R.A.T.T.—living here on state land, next to a mobile-home dealership that the people who drank craft cocktails last night in East Austin see only from a distance on their way to the airport—have built is a *refugee camp* for a particularly American kind of refugee. Maybe they are, as Mollica says, victims of "structural inequities in our society"—refugees from heartless American capitalism. Maybe they are refugees from the notionally well-meaning and certainly well-heeled lifestyle liberalism of Austin (and San Francisco, and Seattle, and so forth), where the Bernie Bros and Elizabeth Warren donors flit between English-usage crusades and sexual crusades and social-justice crusades, with breaks for meals at Jeffrey's (Petrossian caviar, 50g, $300) and Oaxacan Negronis at Midnight Cowboy (make a reservation, and be sure to turn off your cell phone), while keeping a careful and not entirely dissatisfied eye on soaring local property values. Certainly some of the homeless have been failed by our lamentably dysfunctional mental-health system, which has been hobbled both by shallow liberationist *who-are-we-to-judge?* counterculture attitudes and by the anti-tax penny-pinching that has piggybacked on it.

But there's something else happening here, too: These are refugees from America *anno Domini* 2020, Americans who cannot or simply will not deal with the complexities and administrative burdens of modern life, whether those are the bureaucratic intricacies of the welfare state or the lack of subsistence-wage jobs for people who cannot quite bring themselves to be punctual, polite, or halfway respectable-looking. They've always been there, but the contrast grows sharper next to the burgeoning prosperity and ever-more-precious early-empire refinement of cities such as Austin. The philanthropists behind Mobile Loaves &

Fishes have built a "village" outside of Austin in which the homeless can rent tiny houses and trailers, with many of them earning their rent money from on-site jobs. Their hearts are in the right place, but what they are building isn't a village any more than Camp R.A.T.T. is a town—these are *reservations* for poor people, a way to keep America's twenty-first-century misfits and zero-marginal-product workers from taking a dump on the sidewalk in front of places with good breakfast tacos or "plant-based meals" or locally brewed pilsners. The people who are fighting and winning the class war in these United States have Bernie Sanders campaign signs in front of their tastefully modern $1.5 million *Dwell*-worthy East Austin homes. Rich white progressive America is America without mercy.

From the credit-reporting system to the criminal justice system, our country, generous and dynamic as it often is, can be a remarkably *unforgiving* place: Try renting an apartment from the kind and gentle and empathetic people in Austin with a felony conviction on your curriculum vitae, even if it is twenty years old, or as a fifty-year-old marginally employed man without any real convincing or solid references. The self-congratulatory Keep Austin Weird ethic looks very odd indeed, and contemptible, too, when it is coldly contemplated from the intersection where Montopolis Drive meets the Bastrop Highway, on a lovely cloudless Austin winter morning as a white Bentley Continental (those Volkswagens no longer adequately represent Austin's *nouveaux riches*) goes zooming toward the airport, whooshing past the wretched unassimilated old man panhandling on the corner, silent and stoical and signifying exactly what he intends with his big dirty placard reading "Running on Empty."

Death of a Fucking Salesman

New York, New York

A FEW YEARS AGO, Al Pacino starred in a revival of David Mamet's *Glengarry Glen Ross*, and the casting was poignant: In 1992, a much younger and more vigorous Pacino had played the role of hotshot salesman Ricky Roma in the film adaptation of the play; in the Broadway revival, a seventy-two-year-old Pacino played the broken-down has-been Shelley Levene.

Glengarry Glen Ross is the *Macbeth* of real estate, full of great, blistering lines and soliloquies so liberally peppered with profanity that the original cast had nicknamed the show "Death of a Fucking Salesman." But a few of those attending the New York revival left disappointed. For a certain type of young man, the star of *Glengarry Glen Ross* is the character called Blake, played in the film by Alec Baldwin. We know that his name is Blake only from the credits; asked his name by one of the other salesmen, he answers: "What's my name? Fuck you. That's my name." In the film, Blake sets things in motion by delivering a motivational speech and announcing a sales competition: "First prize is a Cadillac Eldorado. Second prize? A set of steak knives. Third prize is, you're fired. Get the picture?" He berates the salesmen in terms both financial—"My watch cost more than your car!"—and sexual. Their problem, in Blake's telling, isn't that they've had a run of bad luck or bad sales leads—or that the real estate they're trying to sell is crap—it's that they aren't real men.

> The leads are weak? You're weak. . . . Your name is "you're wanting," and you can't play the man's game. You can't close them? Then tell your wife your troubles, because only one thing counts in this world: Get them to sign on the line which is dotted. Got that, you fucking faggots?

A few young men waiting to see the show were quoting Blake's speech to one another. For them, and for a number of men who imagine themselves to be hard-hitting competitors (I've never met a woman of whom this is true), Blake's speech is practically a creed. It's one of those things that some guys memorize. But Blake does not appear in the play, the scene having been written specifically for the film and specifically for Alec Baldwin, a sop to investors who feared that the film would not be profitable and wanted an additional jolt of star power to enliven it.

That's some fine irony: Blake's paean to salesmanship was written to satisfy salesmen who did not quite buy David Mamet's original pitch. The play is, if anything, darker and more terrifying without Blake, leaving the poor feckless salesmen at the mercy of a faceless malevolence offstage rather than some ordinary jerk in a BMW. So a few finance bros went home disappointed that they did not get the chance to sing along, as it were, with their favorite hymn.

These guys don't want to see Alec Baldwin in *Glengarry Glen Ross.* What they want is to be Blake. They want to swagger, to curse, to insult, and to exercise power over men, exercising power over men being the classical means to the end of exercising power over women, which is of course what this, and nine-tenths of everything else in human affairs, is about. Blake is a specimen of that famous creature, the "alpha male," and establishing and advertising one's alpha creds is an obsession for some sexually unhappy contemporary men. There is a whole weird little ecosystem of websites (some of them very amusing) and pickup-artist manuals offering men tips on how to be more alpha, more dominant, more commanding, a literature that performs roughly the same function in the lives of these men that *Cosmopolitan* sex tips play in the lives of insecure women. Of course this advice produces cartoonish behavior. If you're wondering where Anthony Scaramucci learned to talk and behave like such a *scaramuccia*, ask him how many times he's seen *Glengarry Glen Ross*.

What's notable about the advice offered to young men aspiring to be "alpha males" is that it is consistent with the classic salesmanship advice offered by the real-world versions of Blake in a hundred thousand business-inspiration books (Og Mandino's *The Greatest Salesman in the World* is the classic of the genre) and self-help tomes, summarized in an old Alcoholics Anonymous slogan: "Fake it 'til you make it." For the pickup artists, the idea is that acting in social situations as though one were confident, successful, and naturally masterful is a pretty good substitute for being those things. Never mind the advice of Cicero (*esse quam videri*, be rather than seem)—just go around acting like Blake and people will treat you like Blake.

If that sounds preposterous, remind yourself who the president of the United States of America is.

Trump is the political version of a pickup artist, and America went to bed with him convinced that he was something other than what he is. Trump inherited his fortune but describes himself as though he were a self-made man.

He has had a middling career in real estate and a poor one as a hotelier and casino operator but convinced people he is a titan of industry. He has never managed a large, complex corporate enterprise, but he did play an executive on a reality show. He presents himself as a confident ladies' man but is so insecure that he invented an imaginary friend to lie to the New York press about his love life and is now married to a woman who is open and blasé about the fact that she married him for his money. He fixates on certain words ("negotiator") and certain classes of words (mainly adjectives and adverbs, "bigly," "major," "world-class," "top," and superlatives), but he isn't much of a negotiator, manager, or leader. He cannot negotiate a health-care deal among members of a party desperate for one, cannot manage his own factionalized and leak-ridden White House, and cannot lead a political movement that aspires to anything greater than the service of his own pathetic vanity.

He wants to be John Wayne, but what he is is "Woody Allen without the humor." Peggy Noonan, to whom we owe that observation, has his number: He is soft, weak, whimpering, and petulant.[1] He isn't smart enough to do the job and isn't man enough to own up to the fact. For all his gold-plated toilets, he is at heart that middling junior salesman watching *Glengarry Glen Ross* and thinking to himself: "That's the man I want to be." How many times do you imagine he has stood in front of a mirror trying to project like Alec Baldwin? Unfortunately for the president, it's Baldwin who does the good imitation of Trump, not the other way around.

Hence the cartoon tough-guy act. Scaramucci's star didn't fade when he gave that batty and profane interview in which he reimagined Steve Bannon as a kind of autoerotic yogi. That's Scaramucci's best impersonation of the sort of man the president of these United States, God help us, aspires to be.

But he isn't that guy. He isn't Blake. He's poor sad old Shelley Levene, who cannot close the deal, who spends his nights whining about the unfairness of it all.

So, listen up, Team Trump: "Put that coffee down. Coffee is for closers only."

Got that?

Adventures in
National Socialism

Marshalltown, Iowa

"**A**LL FOREIGN-MADE VEHICLES PARK IN DESIGNATED AREA in rear of building." So reads the sign in front of United Auto Workers Local 893 in Marshalltown, Iowa, though nobody is bothered much about the CNN satellite truck out front, a Daimler-AG Freightliner proudly declaring itself "Powered by Mercedes-Benz," nor about the guys doggedly and earnestly unpacking yard signs and fifteen-dollar T-shirts and rolls of giveaway stickers from a newish Subaru, all that swag bearing the face and/or logo of Senator Bernie Sanders, the confessing socialist from Brooklyn representing Vermont in the Senate who is, in his half-assed and almost endearingly low-rent way, challenging Hillary Rodham Clinton for the Democratic presidential nomination. The bumper stickers on the mainly foreign-made cars of his followers tell the story: one of those "Peace" (not the more popular "Coexist") slogans made of various world religious symbols, "Clean Water Is for Life!" and "The Warren Wing of the Democratic Party," sundry half-literate denunciations of "Corporate Oligarchy" . . . "Not Just Gay—Ecstatic!"

The union hall was chosen with calculation. Bernie—he's "Bernie," not Senator Sanders or Mr. Sanders or that weirdo socialist from Soviet Beninjerristan, just lovable, cuddly "Bernie," like a grumpy Muppet who

spent too much time around the Workers World Party back in the day—
our Bernie may not be the slickest practitioner of the black arts of elec-
tioneering, but he's got some smart people on his small team, and they
are smart enough to book him in rooms with capacities that are about
85 percent of the modest crowds they are expecting, thereby creating the
illusion of overflow audiences. They do all the usual tedious stuff, such
as planting volunteers in the audience to shout on cue, "Yes, yes!" and
the occasional Deanesque "YEAAAAAAAH!" It's all very familiar. Sanders, as stiff a member as the Senate has to offer, repeatedly refers to the
audience as "brothers and sisters," and the union bosses greet one
another as "brother," and you get the feeling that after a beer or three
one of these characters is going to slip up and let out a "comrade."

If it's anybody, it's probably going to be the grandmotherly lady in
the hammer-and-sickle T-shirt. She's well inclined toward Bernie, she
says, though she distrusts his affiliation with the Democratic Party. "He's
part of . . . *them*," she says, grimacing. "Yeah," says her friend, who stops
to think for a moment. "He's a senator, right?"

Aside from Grandma Stalin there, there's not a lot of overtly Soviet
iconography on display around the Bernieverse, but the word "socialism"
is on a great many lips. Not Bernie's lips, for heaven's sake: The guy's running for president. But Tara Monson, a young mother who has come out
to the UAW hall to support her candidate, is pretty straightforward about
her issues: "Socialism," she says. "My husband's been trying to get me to
move to a socialist country for years—but now, maybe, we'll get it here."
The socialist country she has in mind is Norway, which of course isn't a
socialist country at all: It's an oil emirate. Monson is a classic American
radical, which is to say, a wounded teenager in an adult's body: Asked
what drew her to socialism and Bernie, she says that she is "very atheist"—*very?*—and that her Catholic parents were not accepting of this. She
goes on to cite her "social views," and by the time she gets around to the
economic questions, she's not Helle Thorning-Schmidt—she's Pat
Buchanan, complaining about "sending our jobs overseas."

L'Internationale, my Whig patootie. This is *national* socialism.

IN THE BERNIEVERSE, there's a whole lot of nationalism mixed up in the socialism. Bernie Sanders is, in fact, leading a national-socialist movement, which is a queasy and uncomfortable thing to write about a man who is the son of Jewish immigrants from Poland and whose family was largely wiped out in the Holocaust. But there is no other adequate way to characterize his views and his politics. The incessant reliance on xenophobic (and largely untrue) tropes blaming the current economic woes of the United States on scheming foreigners, especially the wicked Chinese, "stealing our jobs" and victimizing his class allies is nothing more than an updated version of Kaiser Wilhelm II's "yellow peril" rhetoric, and though the kaiser had a more poetical imagination—he said he had a vision of the Buddha riding a dragon across Europe, laying waste to all—Bernie's take is substantially similar. He describes the normalization of trade relations with China as "catastrophic"—Sanders and Jesse Helms both voted against the Clinton-backed China-trade legislation—and heaps scorn on every other trade-liberalization pact. That economic interactions with foreigners are inherently hurtful and immoral is central to his view of how the world works.

Bernie bellows that he remembers a time when you could walk into a department store and "buy things made in the U.S.A." Before the "Made in China" panic, there was the "Made in Japan" panic of the 1950s and 1960s, and the products that provoked that panic naturally went on to be objects of nostalgia. (A quarter-century ago, the artist Roger Handy published a book of photographs titled *Made in Japan: Transistor Radios of the 1950s and 1960s.*) There was a "Made in Taiwan" panic, and there will be a "Made in India" panic, too. There already is, really: Workers made in India scare the bejesus out of mediocre tech guys in California.

Like most of these advocates of "economic patriotism" (Barack Obama's favored phrase), Bernie worries a great deal about trade with brown people—Asians, Latin Americans—but has never, so far as public records show, made so much as a peep about our very large trade deficit with Sweden, which as a share of bilateral trade volume is about the same as our trade deficit with China, or about the size of our trade deficit with Canada, our largest trading partner. Sanders doesn't rail about the Canadians stealing our jobs—his ire is reserved almost exclusively for the Chinese and the Mexicans, as when he demanded of Hillary Rodham Clinton, in the words of the old protest song, "Which side are you on?" The bad guys, or American workers "seeing their jobs go to China or Mexico?"

But for the emerging national socialist, dusky people abroad are not the only problem. I speak with Bernie volunteer McKinly Springer, an earnest young man whose father worked for the UAW local hosting the rally. He's very interested in policies that interpose the government between employers and employees—for example, mandatory paid maternity and paternity leave. He lived for a time in Germany, first studying abroad and then working for Bosch, an automotive-parts company. He is a great admirer of the German welfare state, saying: "I ask myself: Why do they have these nice things, and we can't?" I ask him to answer his own question, and his answer is at once familiar and frightening: "Germany is very homogeneous. They have lots of white people. We're very diverse. We have the melting pot, and that's a big struggle."

"My struggle" in German is *Mein Kampf.*

That the relative success of the Western European welfare states, and particularly of the Scandinavian states, is rooted in cultural and ethnic homogeneity is a long-standing conservative criticism of Bernie-style schemes to recreate the Danish model in New Jersey and Texas and Mississippi. The conservative takeaway is: Don't build a Scandinavian welfare state in Florida. But if you understand the challenges of diversity and you still want to build a Scandinavian welfare state, or at least a German one, that points to some uncomfortable conclusions. Indeed, one very worked-up young man confronts Bernie angrily about his apparent unwillingness to speak up more robustly about his liberal views on illegal immigration. Springer gets a few sentences into a disquisition on ethnic homogeneity when a shadow crosses his face, as though he is for the first time thinking through the ugly implications of what he believes in light of what he knows. He trails off, looking troubled.

Bernie, who represents the second-whitest state in the union, may not have thought too hard about this. But the Left is thinking about it: T. A. Frank, writing in the *New Republic*, argues that progressives should oppose Obama's immigration-reform plans because poor foreigners flooding our labor markets will undercut the wages of low-income Americans. Cheap foreign cars, cheap foreign labor—you can see the argument.

"CONSERVATIVES CAN IDENTIFY EACH OTHER BY SMELL—did you know that?" He's an older gentleman, neatly dressed in a pink button-down shirt, his slightly unruly white hair and cracked demeanor calling to mind the presidential candidate he is here to evaluate. He's dead serious, too, and it's not just Republicans' sniffing one another's butts that's on his mind. He goes on a good-humored tirade about how one can identify conservatives' and progressives' homes simply by walking down the street and observing the landscaping. Conservatives, he insists, "torture" the flowers and shrubbery, imposing strict order and conformity on their yards, whereas progressives just let things bloom as nature directs. I am tempted to ask him which other areas in life he thinks might benefit from that kind of unregulated, spontaneous order, but I think better of it. One of Sanders's workers, a young Occupy veteran, shoots me an eye-rolling look: Crazy goes with the territory.

Here in a dreary, run-down, hideous little corner of Des Moines dotted with dodgy-looking bars and dilapidated grocery stores advertising their willingness to accept EBT payments sits Drake University, where Bernie is speaking at Sheslow Auditorium, a kind of mock church—spire, stained glass, double staircase leading down to the podium for communion—that is the perfect setting for the mock-religious fervor that the senator brings to the stump. He is a clumsy speaker, pronouncing "oligarchy"—a word he uses in every speech—as though he were starting to say "à la mode" or "Allahu akbar!" He's one of those rhetorical oafs

whose only dynamic modulations are radical sudden shifts in volume—
he's the oratorical equivalent of every Nirvana song ever written—and
he is undisciplined, speaking for an hour and then pressing right through,
on and on, feeling the need to check off every progressive box, as though
new orbiters in the Bernieverse might think him a Rick Santorum–level
pro-lifer if he didn't lay his pro-choice credentials out on the table at least
once during every speech. "Brothers and sisters . . ." repeatedly: global
warming, fifteen-dollar minimum wage, putting an end to free trade,
gays, gays, abortion, gays, lies about women making only seventy-eight
cents on the male dollar, mass transit, gays and abortion and gays, Kochs
and Waltons and hedge-fund managers!

And gays!

He does not suggest that conservatives can literally sniff one another
out pheromonally, but the idea that his political opponents are a tribe
apart is central to his platform, which can be summarized in three words:
"Us and Them." And, contra the hammer-and-sickle lady, Bernie is
pretty emphatic that he is not one of the hated Them.

And this is where the Bernieverse is really off-kilter, where the intellectual shallowness of the man and his followers is as impossible to miss
as a winter bonfire. The Scandinavian welfare states they so admire are
very different from the United States in many ways, and one of the most
important is that their politics are consensus-driven. That has some
significant downsides, prominent among them the crushing conformity
that is ruthlessly enforced in practically every aspect of life. (The Dano-
Norwegian novelist Aksel Sandemose called it "Jante law," after the petty
and bullying social milieu of the fictional village Jante in *A Fugitive
Crosses His Tracks*.) But it is also a stabilizing and moderating force in
politics, allowing for the emergence of a subtle and sophisticated and
remarkably broad social agreement that contains political disputes.
Bernie's politics, on the other hand, are the polar opposite of Scandinavian: He promises not just confrontation but hostile, theatrical confrontation, demonizing not only his actual opponents but his perceived
enemies as well, including the Walton family, whose members are not

particularly active in politics these days, and some of whom are notably liberal. That doesn't matter: If they have a great deal of wealth, they are the enemy. (What about Tom Steyer and George Soros? "False equivalency," Bernie scoffs.) He knows who Them is: the Koch brothers, who make repeated appearances in every speech; scheming foreigners who are stealing our jobs; bankers, the traditional bogeymen of conspiracy theorists ranging from Father Coughlin and Henry Ford to Louis Farrakhan; Wall Street; and so forth.

He is steeped in this stuff, having begun his political career with the radical Liberty Union Party in the 1970s. Liberty Union sometimes ran its own candidates but generally endorsed candidates from other parties, most often the Socialist Party USA, making a few exceptions: twice for Lenora Fulani's New Alliance Party and once for the Workers World Party, a Communist party that split with Henry Wallace's Progressives over its view of Mao Zedong's murderous rule and the Soviet Union's invasion of Hungary—both of which it supported. The radical political language of the 1970s and 1980s spoke of a capitalist conspiracy or a conspiracy of bankers (a conspiracy of Jewish bankers, in the ugliest versions), a notion to which Sanders pays ongoing tribute with the phrase "rigged economy."

His pose is not the traditional progressive managerial-empiricist posture but a moral one. He is very fond of the word "moral"—"moral imperative," "moral disaster," "moral crisis"—and those who see the world differently are not, in his estimate, guilty of misunderstanding, or ignorance, or bad judgment: They are guilty of "crimes."

And criminalizing things is very much on Bernie's agenda, beginning with political dissent. At every event he swears to introduce a constitutional amendment reversing Supreme Court decisions that affirmed the free-speech protections of people and organizations filming documentaries, organizing web campaigns, and airing television commercials in the hopes of influencing elections or public attitudes toward public issues. That this would amount to a repeal of the First Amendment does not trouble Bernie at all. If the First Amendment enables Them, then the First Amendment has got to go.

F. A. HAYEK'S *ROAD TO SERFDOM* NOTWITHSTANDING, corralling off foreign-made cars does not lead inevitably to corralling off foreign-born people or members of ethnic minorities, although the Asians-and-Latinos-with-their-filthy-cheap-goods rhetoric in and around the Bernieverse is troubling. But there are many kinds of Us-and-Them politics, and Bernie Sanders, to be sure, is not a national socialist in the mode of Alfred Rosenberg or Julius Streicher.

He is a national socialist in the mode of Hugo Chávez. He isn't driven by racial hatred; he's driven by political hatred. And that's bad enough.

"This is not about me," Bernie is fond of saying. Instead, he insists, it's about building a grassroots movement that will be in a permanent state of "political revolution"—his words—against the people he identifies as class enemies: Kochs, Waltons, Republicans, bankers, Wall Street, Them—the numerically inferior Them. His views are totalitarian, inasmuch as there is no aspect of life that he believes to be beyond the reach of the state, and they are deeply illiberal inasmuch as he is willing to jettison a great deal of American liberalism—including freedom of speech—if doing so means that he can stifle his enemies' ability to participate in the political process. He rejects John F. Kennedy's insistence that "a rising tide lifts all boats"—and he is willing to sink as many boats as is necessary in his crusade against the reality that some people make more money than others.

Part of this is just a parting sentimental gesture from a daft old man (Occupy Geritol!)—soupy feel-good identity politics for aging McGovernites and dopey youngsters in Grateful Dead T-shirts. That an outlier of a senator from Vermont wants to organize American politics as a permanent domestic war on unpopular minorities is, while distasteful, probably not that important.

That Hillary Rodham Clinton said the same thing in Des Moines a day later, on the other hand, is significant, and terrifying—in part because it's batshit crazy, in part because Hillary Rodham by-God Clinton is, incredibly enough, to the right of Donald Trump on trade and to the Trumpkin Republicans' libertarian side on much else. As economist

Bryan Caplan once said to me, the United States does not have a classical-liberal party: It has two moderate national-socialist parties, one a little more nationalist, the other a little more socialist.

Farming Dirty

Valley Springs, South Dakota

"I'M FARMING DIRTY!" says Kevin Scott, a father of six with one of those delightful Marge Gunderson Upper Midwestern tundra accents, who out here in his little house on the prairie right down the road from *that* little house on the prairie—the one Laura Ingalls Wilder wrote about—is living the simple farmer's life, which in the early twenty-first century includes such combat-derived technologies as surveillance drones and satellite overheads, along with giant tractors decked out with multiple touch-screen arrays, into which are pumped vast quantities of real-time corn-and-soybean-related data of various kinds, and sensors and GPS tracking doohickeys and a vast pneumatic seeding apparatus that no longer scatters the seed upon the ground in onanistically incontinent fashion but places *this* individual piece of specially treated seed corn right *there*, just exactly 1.75 inches below the surface and topped with a little dollop of fertilizer, just so, cleanly and precisely, every nine inches, sixteen rows at a time in a forty-foot sweep. There are five grains of untreated kernels in every hundred—just enough to keep from breeding pesticide-resistant pests. "I can monitor this from my cell phone in Washington," Scott says, and that's a part of this farmer's life now, too: the meetings in Washington or Dallas or Paris and the trade shows in

Orange County and San Antonio, the calls with the secretary of agriculture and his staff, monitoring the political chatter and commodity futures. His customers are Chinese pig farmers, his competitors are in Brazil and Argentina, he and his fellow soybean and corn producers have problems from Brussels to Beijing.

But what's really vexing Kevin Scott today is the million-dollar arsenal of high-tech farm implements sitting idle in his barn doing no farming at all, doing jack all, just sitting there depreciating. In this part of South Dakota, the farmers have planted only about 5 percent of their soybean crop and 25 percent of their corn. They like to plant corn by April 20. This year, it was still snowing in May, and since then it's been rain and rain and rain and rain, the Big Sioux River looking very big indeed, spilling over its banks. The highway medians look like Florida alligator swamps and there's weeks of rain ponding all over the place, standing in the fields, halfway up trees in some places, making it too wet to plant.

After a severe drought a few years back, years of soft farm prices, and a trade war in which Beijing has jammed its collective hand right up the hickory-striped overalls of American farmers and taken a firm icy grip on their scrota in retaliation for President Trump's punitive tariffs on Chi-Comm imports, now *this*, this Coleridgean nightmare of water, water everywhere. Farmers used to pray for rain. Now, they are praying that it will stop long enough to let them put in their crops. Corn prices are high and rising . . . because nobody can plant corn. So farmers will either miss out on the bull market or be forced into speculation, selling crops they haven't planted yet and may end up not being able to deliver, putting them at the risk of getting woefully and dangerously upside-down on those contracts.

Decisions. Kevin Scott looks out the window. Rain.

Things have been getting stuck in the mud so much that Scott has just left the tow rope tied to the front of his biggest tractor, the one with the tank-style rolling treads instead of the man-high tires, knowing that something else is going to have to be pulled out.

Farming dirty, indeed.

What "farming dirty" actually means is leaving the old corn stalks mulching on the fields when the next crop is planted instead of cleaning them off. It is an ecologically sound practice, but Scott, who says "There is a place for things" like a man who really means it, does not like the messy look of farming dirty. He points to some evenly and uniformly bear-colored fields of artfully plowed Houdek loam. (Does *your* state have an official state soil? Because South Dakota has an official state soil, and it is Houdek loam.) "I'd prefer my fields to look like that," he says, with a little bit of gentle lamentation. "But this is a good way to plant."

Scott is on the board of the American Soybean Association and sits on its governing committee; its trade, policy, and international-affairs committee; and its biotech working group. He represents the ASA on a railroad business council, because those soybeans are not getting to China on magic carpets. He's a national policy adviser for his state soybean association, too, and was its president for a decade. (Term limits: The South Dakota Soybean Association has them.) And his policy agenda is free trade.

This is Trump country, and the farmers here are the kind of conservative that usually gets described as *staunch* or *rock-ribbed* or something like that. Get them talking about trade, though, and they're Manchester liberals. The farmers were on the opposite side of the free-trade debate during the controversy over the Corn Laws, but now they are frank and unapologetic and assertive owners of that most hated of all Trump-country epithets.

Globalists. Down on the farm.

SO, HERE'S THE THING ABOUT SOYBEANS. Americans produce beaucoup soybeans. Brazil and Argentina, being in the Southern Hemisphere, produce gigantic crops in the U.S. off-season. China has a powerful hunger for soybeans, albeit a mostly indirect one. Two kinds of creatures walking this earth really like eating soybeans: pigs and hippies. Chinese people do eat soybeans, too, but what the nouveau riche Chinese palate has a real taste for just now is *pork* and, to a lesser extent, chicken. That's a pretty predictable thing following a pretty familiar pattern: When poor countries become less poor—though with a per capita GDP of less than $9,000 a year, down there with Cuba and Kazakhstan, China is by no means a rich country—the first thing the people usually spend their newly disposable income on is more and better food, which in much of the world means more and better animal protein.

The world is hungry for protein, and the American heartland is the Saudi Arabia, the De Beers, and the Fire Creek gold mine of protein, including soy protein. Kevin Scott's soy protein comes out of the ground, goes into the hopper and then down to the silo, rides the rails from South Dakota to the Pacific Northwest or the Gulf of Mexico, is loaded into shipping containers or massive PANAMAX bulk carriers, some of which are specially outfitted for carrying grains or soybeans with their hulls sloped at forty-five degrees to make stevedoring easier, and then continues on to ports around the world, Chinese ports such as those at Dalian and Nantong prominent among them. At some point along the way, the beans get ground into meal, and that meal goes into animal feed—down the gullets of Chinese chickens or, more likely, into the monogastric digestive tract of a Chinese pig. And thence into the butcher's case at whatever the Chinese answer to Piggly Wiggly or Whole Foods or Albertsons is. That's what used to happen. That's what's *supposed* to happen.

And along came Trump.

Donald Trump is obsessed with the so-called trade deficit—a confusing term used to mislead the lightly informed about the phenomenon in question—and he has been obsessed with it since Ross Perot's "giant sucking sound" was a thing. Trade, not illegal immigration, is Trump's longest-standing hobbyhorse. And when he got into Washington, he rode that hobbyhorse all over town, leaving a trail of the stuff horses leave trails of. The first thing he did was kill the Trans-Pacific Partnership, a trade alliance that would have made the United States an important member of a bloc *intentionally constructed* to counter Chinese dominance in the Pacific Rim. Soybean prices tanked. Trump went on to impose punitive tariffs on steel and aluminum imports, including those from the European Union and Canada. He ordered 25 percent duties on more than eight hundred categories of Chinese goods. After the failed trade negotiations with China, he ordered higher tariffs on another $200 billion of Chinese goods. The Chinese retaliated with tariffs on, among other things, U.S. soybeans—which had long been the biggest U.S. export to China after aircraft.

One of the nice things about being a totalitarian police state is that you can do things like just order your soybean importers not to do business with American producers, and that is what China has quietly done. Beijing has, in fact, been following a clever strategy. Its tariffs on and soft boycott of U.S. soybeans drove down U.S. soybean prices in absolute terms but also relative to producers in Brazil and other nations. Beijing then authorized its buyers to pick up those cheap U.S. soybeans as part of a program to replenish long-term reserves—which means that they can be imported without payment of the 25 percent tariff. Which is to say, U.S. producers suffered the consequences of the tariff, but Chinese buyers did not have to pay higher prices. China canceled billions of dollars in planned soybean purchases. By early this year, soybean prices were near decade lows. From 2016 to 2018, the value of U.S. soybean exports to China dropped by nearly 75 percent, according to G. William Hoagland of the Bipartisan Policy Center.

The steel used to make farm equipment? That got more expensive. So did many other inputs, from fertilizer to chemicals.

In 2013, U.S. farm income was $123 billion. This year, it is forecast to come in at less than $70 billion. President Trump is going to have a rough time of it going into rural America and asking farmers whether they are better off today than they were four years ago—the numbers do not bear that out.

And that is not a problem that stays on the farm. Sioux Falls, South Dakota, is a vibrant little city, one of those midwestern gems such as

Kansas City and Grand Rapids that punch above their weight. Its downtown has the feel of being a couple of years past the apex of a pretty successful revitalization project—you know the scene: wine bars, ambitious little restaurants, those funny shops that always seem to stock three not *obviously* related categories of product—like scented candles, stationery, and petite little bottles of balsamic vinegar—that make you wonder how on earth they generate enough revenue to pay the rent. It is nice, and there's a theater and people on the sidewalks and drunk young women on those sip-'n'-ride contraptions that are one part mobile cocktail party, one part tandem bicycle that look like a lawsuit just waiting to happen. But this urbane little core is built on soybeans and other farm products.

"It affects everything," says Scott VanderWal, a fourth-generation South Dakota farmer and the vice president of the American Farm Bureau Federation. (The president of the American Farm Bureau Federation is a Georgia farmer who rejoices in the name "Zippy Duvall.") VanderWal is a kind of farmer-wonk-diplomat whose office is so thoroughly out in the country that it doesn't have an actual address. He just gives you the address to the nearest place that has one, which is a modest little house guarded by a dog that looks like it could have been an extra on *Game of Thrones*, and then stands outside and watches for whoever looks lost. A bad year for farmers is a bad year for a lot of people around here. "It affects ag services, obviously," he says. "But it also affects Main Street businesses. It affects the flower shop and the furniture store. If farmers don't have any money in our pockets, we aren't out spending it."

They appreciate that fact in town, too.

"We all live on farm dollars," says a construction-supply salesman drinking an after-work Grain Belt–brand beer at a Sioux Falls bar with a sign that says there's a two-drink minimum if you want to *cash your payroll check at the bar*. It's not too far from a place with a sign straightforwardly offering "African Food and Cold Beer." Out there in weird old red-Pontiac, leg-tattoo Middle America—which starts only a few blocks away from the cute little wine bars and the Orpheum

Theater—the sense of prosperity is not what you would call *evenly distributed*. Sioux Falls is infested with ghastly little hut casinos about the size and shape and smell of a not-very-well-run 7-Eleven, basically downscale adult daycare centers with adult video games. The farmers themselves seem to be a pretty thrifty, hustling, entrepreneurial bunch, but the edges of the local economies in communities such as this do not have a lot of room for error. Sioux Falls is nearly 90 percent white, and almost a third of the adults are college graduates. The median household income is just a little under the national average, but the cost of living is low. At the same time, Sioux Falls has a number of familiar problems, heroin and opioid use prominent among them. The number of drug-overdose deaths in the county *doubled* from 2017 to 2018, and it is expected to grow even more this year. The dead were overwhelmingly men, forty-three years old on average.

THE GRAYBEARDS AROUND HERE have seen what a bad farm economy really looks like. They saw it in the 1980s, when 20 percent interest rates crippled the financing-dependent agricultural sector. With farm income already taking a beating, the collateral damage from the trade war could very well have effects that will linger long after trade relations return to whatever is going to count as normal from here on out.

People are nice here. Not Minnesota nice—the real thing. Kevin Scott worries that the stress from his advocacy work and the frustration of being sidelined by the weather—with all the financial and professional complications that brings with it—might be making him a little bit cranky at home. His wife assures me this is not the case. "He does everything he can," she says. "Eventually, that's it. You do what you can, and trust God for the rest." There's a little sign in the kitchen, and it doesn't say "Bless This House" or "Let Go and Let God" or anything like that. It says: "No Whining." Scott's son, who has recently joined him in the business, is the fifth generation of his family to work that land. His great-great-grandfather helped to found the Methodist church up the hill. It's raining, and there are grasshoppers to worry about, and nematodes, and aphids. He's proud to be a farmer. He says he likes producing something that's real, that people need. *No whining.*

They want to keep doing this. Kevin Scott talks about a meeting with some of his French counterparts a few years ago. They warned him not to let the United States go the way of France, where government takes the leading role in agriculture, micromanaging farming and dictating to farmers. "What they have in France, he said, is a 'farm museum.' Not farming."

The truth is, even if none of these nice people will exactly say it, that none of them really likes doing business with the Chinese. The Chinese make promises and break them. They negotiate agreements and then back out of them. And the shenanigans—you would not believe the shenanigans. Everybody knows about the Chinese penchant for stealing intellectual property, but it isn't limited to smartphones and automotive technology. In 2013, seven Chinese agents were arrested digging up experimental seeds from Iowa cornfields, planning to ship them back to China for examination and replication. The cell targeted products from Monsanto, Dupont Pioneer, and LG Seeds. The leader of the group was employed by Beijing Dabeinong Technology Group, a private firm that received funding from the Chinese government for "science and technology" research. Crazy stuff.

Broken promises, agreements reneged on, playing fast and loose with the rules, shameless rapacity: China is a nation of Trumps, and even Trump doesn't want to do business with them.

But it is a funny old world. The Chinese are a pain in the ass and worse, but there are a whole lot of them, and they are hungry hungry hungry, and the United States is the world's superlative agricultural producer. We produce so much that we don't know what to do with it all. The soybean guys have spent years traveling the world teaching hog farmers and chicken mechanics how to improve their businesses and incorporate modern agricultural practices, expanding their own market by helping producers abroad to build up their own local markets. The American Soybean Association had an office in Beijing for twenty-five years before a single shipload of beans went to China. This stuff takes work.

It is also an interdependent world. There's a terrible outbreak of swine fever rampaging through Chinese pork country right now. According to official estimates, more hogs have died from the outbreak than the ginormous U.S. pork industry produces in a year, and the smart little piggies think Beijing is probably lowballing that number. As VanderWal says, that means that even if U.S.–Chinese soybean trade goes back to normal, there may not be much of a Chinese market left to sell into. Dead hogs eat no beans.

The silver lining is that with China temporarily turning up its nose at American soybeans, those soybeans are available to other markets—often at a nice introductory price that the farmers hope will go up. In some cases, ships bound for Chinese ports have been redirected while at sea. (One ship even sat outside a Chinese port for days and days as the authorities decided whether they were going to allow it to go ashore: stateless beans!) So the U.S. soybean guys have been knocking on doors and shaking hands and making friends in Egypt, Algeria, Morocco, and in Europe, too. They don't talk pork very much in the Muslim countries, but there's chicken and beef to be fed, and the French love their *rillettes de porc*. Scott hopes that the U.S. soybean industry will come out of this with a more diversified market and a less China-dependent one. But getting there will be a long and difficult process—and it's going to be a hell of a lot harder if the soybean farmers don't have any money to work with.

Farming is a business of relationships, VanderWal says, and it is critical that U.S. farmers be regarded as "reliable suppliers." It took years for American farmers' reputations to recover from the debacle of the Soviet grain embargo, a daft and botched attempt to starve the Russians into penance for invading Afghanistan, cooked up by the great peacemaker Jimmy Carter and rescinded by the purported warmonger Ronald Reagan. The costs of the embargo were borne almost entirely by American farmers: The Russians just bought more grain from Argentina. VanderWal fears that the current situation may damage U.S. farmers' reputation for being reliable suppliers. The Bernie Sanders Left is at least as hostile to trade as is the Trump administration, and if the nation as a whole is turning away from free trade, that cannot help but affect how farmers do business. VanderWal and his group were vocal supporters of the TPP and nervous about renegotiating NAFTA even though there were parts of it that they believed to be in need of reform. But the TPP is gone and it is not coming back. VanderWal believes that the best course of action is to press for bilateral agreements with the TPP countries, along with the European Union and the United Kingdom—"assuming they are ever able to actually break away from the EU." That and the Golden Rule, he says: "Treat others how you'd want to be treated. Stick to the deal. Honor your agreements." He thinks there's room for reform at the World Trade Organization, and he hopes that farmers can get Washington's attention and put all those expensive diplomats to work on new trade deals.

And that includes, ultimately, a deal with China, too. There is not really any way around it. And, in the end, a way around that would not be desirable anyway. The reality is that the world is interdependent, and our institutions should be in accord with that reality.

Farmers are paying the price for somebody else's crusade. This is really not their fight. They're farmers. They don't do drama and hysterics and *Sturm und Drang*: They do business. VanderWal said as much in congressional testimony not long ago: "Farmers are patriots. We were willing to step up and take one for the team. But, at some point . . ."

What's really annoying to farmers is that none of this is really about them. This is about BMWs and Toyotas and steel and Boeing and the fact that Americans don't like seeing "Made in China" on socks and flip-flops they buy at Walmart because we are losing our position of worldwide sock and flip-flop dominance, of front-runner status in the flip-flop race, whatever. "For years, this was a nonpartisan issue," VanderWal says. "I didn't like Bill Clinton very much, but he did a fine job on trade. Obama worked on trade. The president is right about the theft of intellectual property, and we do broadly support what the president is trying to do."

But is it getting done? VanderWal smiles. "The president doesn't respond well to criticism."

BACK AT THE SCOTT FARM, there's an Eisenhower-era Farmall 300 tractor waiting for a new coat of red paint and a restoration. Kevin Scott's office is full of family pictures, including the old-timers as little children back in the 1920s and 1930s, posing in front of old-timey tractors—and pictures of the same men, grown old, posing in front of more modern farm machinery. We talk on a Wednesday. He is expecting another grandchild on Monday. Six children of his own—these farmers are reliable producers, indeed: independent, cheerful, useful.

No whining.

These guys aren't a bunch of Elmers out in the wilderness scratching a living out of the soil. "The soil is our *factory*," Scott says, and his business is capital-intensive, high-tech, and demanding. He could very well be managing a factory or a law firm or a hedge fund or another kind of business. These are smart guys, and more than a few of them *are* in fact managing other businesses, too: They're on the boards of banks and insurance companies, they're involved in real estate, this and that. But they love farming. They love the life and their communities, the way farming and family fit together. They are enthusiasts. One of them tells an old joke about the farmer who wins the lottery and says that he plans to just keep on farming until the money's all gone.

"I want to let people know they need to make their planting decisions and cropping decisions, all production decisions based on where they see the market and where they see their own weather pattern and when they can get into the fields in their own area," says Sonny Perdue, the secretary of agriculture. Translation: Tariff-crippled farmers, don't count on a bailout to make you whole. There's going to be something, yes, but that's just a patch. It is a big wide complex world and, the grand tradition of

U.S. farm policy notwithstanding, a check from the government is not a long-term solution.

It's the tail end of May, and Kevin Scott is in his office looking at the calendar. May 25 was a big day, a red-letter day: That was planting day, not as determined by agronomic considerations or the cereal goddesses or Kevin Scott's own personal sense of time, but as determined by the insurance company. If your crop is insured for x, that figure holds only if it is planted by the date the insurance company determines. After that, the value of your coverage declines by 1 percent every day. Farming is an up-and-down business with very little income security in the best of times, and the worst-case scenario of cashing in the crop insurance dribbles away, 1 percent every twenty-four hours, after planting day. Kevin Scott runs the numbers. He has been farming for thirty-seven years, and he's used his crop insurance only twice. He uses the words "break even" fairly often. He talks about the "prevent plant" option, meaning an arrangement in which a farmer accepts a substantially reduced insurance payment for a crop that is not planted at all. The insurance companies say they are getting more calls about that than they are used to. Farmers are, by necessity, realists. You can't plant when it's raining out and there's water ponding in your cornstalk-littered fields. You can't control a wet, leaden spring of low skies and prairie thunder. And you can't control what's happening in Washington, Beijing, Brussels, the Chicago Board of Trade, Brazil, or the Panama Canal.

What can you do? You can sit in this room, look at these pictures, think about that new grandchild, and—as your predecessors have done for thousands of years—look out on those fields and up at the sky and hope and pray and get back to work.

Among the Flat-Earthers

Frisco, Texas

"AM I JUST DROPPING a garbage bag full of dead dogs into outer space?"

OK, so that question is going to need some context. . . .

And the context, here at the Embassy Suites Hotel Convention Center and Spa on the dreary Cracker Barrel–pocked exurban northern fringe of Dallas, is the Flat Earth International Convention, which—and this is the first thing you need to know and will be enthusiastically reminded of every seven minutes—has *absolutely no relationship of any kind whatsoever* with the Flat Earth Society, those heretical, weak-tea, milk-and-water, pansified, *considerably less respectable* flat-Earth enthusiasts, who, unlike our rambunctious gang here at the Embassy Suites, have basically nothing at all to say about the finer points of Hebrew cosmology, laser-beam experiments disproving the curvature of the Earth, nighttime infrared photography, autographed Illuminati cards, sundry NASA hoaxes ("'NASA' stands for 'Not Always Telling Truths,'" insists one conference-goer as his fellow conferees scratch their heads in pained acronymic perplexation), or any of the other Very High Weirdness on chiropteran display for those willing to fork over the $250 entry fee (cash only at the door, please, because that's not shady-seeming in any way, and here's your hand-scribbled receipt from the harried wife of the guy who runs this show—"Sorry, we're Canadian!" she explains) and enjoy the rich terroir of Embassy Suites coffee and take unselfconscious selfies with a parade of honest-to-God flat-Earth *celebrities* after a couple of intensely awkward audience Q-'n'-A sessions (heavy on the Q, if you know what I mean and I know that you do!) during which a very wide range of semi-debilitating social-anxiety pathologies is on excruciating display.

From the stage, Mark Sargent smiles down over it all—beatific, imperturbable. He is a hero in this world. A Very Big Deal indeed.

And he is trying to wrap his head around those hypothetical canine corpses that may or may not be floating about in space. (Also: "Space Is Fake!" as one seminar title insists.) The guy in the audience wants to know how deep he could dig a dog-burying hole in the purely hypothetical case in which he might find himself obliged to bury a garbage bag full of dead dogs, which he very much has on the brain, for some reason. He is concerned about the possibility of falling through into whatever is on the other side, floating there in space like Major Tom with a Hefty Steel Sak full of dead dog. Sargent, who *unquestionably* has the mien of a man who knows that he is participating in a scam, takes a second. "There is no consensus about how thick the Earth is," he responds. In fact, there is no general agreement here among the flat-Earthers about what the Earth actually looks like, which of several competing maps and models of it might be accurate, or even whether drawing up such a thing is epistemically possible. For a bunch of guys who have organized a two-day international conference about the shape of the Earth, they strangely do not seem to give a furry crack of a rat's patootie what the Earth is shaped like. It's kind of weird.

"All we can do is agree that it's not a globe," Sargent says.

THAT'S ONE OF THE FUNNY THINGS about these flat-Earth guys: They not only don't know a goddamned thing, they don't claim to know or want to know a goddamned thing beyond the one thing that brings them together—the thing about the Earth's being shaped like a ball, a claim they sneer at as an obvious fraud and superstition and hoax put forward by "globalists" to snooker vulnerable believers on behalf of Satan, who has a thing for balls, apparently.

And there is no evading Satan's great swinging balls here. The flatness of the Earth is the big topic on the main stage, but the hot topic on the sidelines is Satanic ritual abuse, the fixation du jour of the QAnon conspiracy nuts who believe that Donald Trump is just right on the verge of leading a massive national purge of Satanic pedophiles, who, as everybody knows, secretly run the world. (Also: *Jews! Jews! Jews!*) As flat-Earth author Noel Hadley tells me, "Satan runs everything: music, Hollywood, media, Republicans, Democrats, Washington, Israel, *Zionism....*" They know Satan when they see him. But they don't know what the Earth looks like—only that it is not round. And that if people only understood that, then they would . . . change their diets. And vaccine companies would go out of business, as one speaker insisted.

"We don't believe in a flying pancake in space," says exasperated conference organizer Robbie Davidson, a Canadian conspiracy hobbyist, "and we don't believe you can fall off the edge of it." But what does the Earth actually look like? That, apparently, needs "more investigation," in the inevitable dodge uttered from the stage. Right outside the door, a guy who looks exactly like a *Lord of the Rings* elf who retired to be an Uber driver in Colorado Springs is nonetheless selling models of the Earth that look an awful lot like a pancake in space—or, really, a dinner plate, since this sad folk art appears to be made of repurposed kitchenware and electric clock motors, with the sun and moon circling the sky on the minute hand in decidedly non-heliocentric fashion. There's a big version up on the stage, too. But just because the world is a dinner plate sitting on top of a battery-operated quartz clock motor doesn't mean that you can fall off the edge—the general consensus here is that Antarctica is actually a giant wall of ice surrounding the flat Earth, making exit impossible.

A bearded man in quasi-clerical garb walks by. Another *Lord of the Rings* elf with a name tag reading "Angel" confers with Elf No. 1. There's a guy on a crutch with a ballcap emblazoned "Level-Headed" and a T-shirt reading "Flat Outta Hell!" arguing with a bouncer, who thinks Crutch Guy may have faked his credentials. The bouncer wants to see some government-issued identification: Funny how these guys suddenly trust The Man when there's conference-goer revenue on the line. Someone across the room denounces the United Nations.

NOEL HADLEY TELLS ME he is interested in Hellenistic mystery religions, and he has written a book on the subject, an extract from which reveals it to be exactly the illiterate effluence you would expect of a self-published flat-Earth tract written by a man whose Amazon page identifies him as "a former career wedding photographer." (It's the word *career* that really gets it done, there, in that particular sentence.) The hilarious part, the wonderful irony, is that for all his sincere interest in mystery cults and his "research" on the subject, he does not quite seem to understand that he has joined a mystery cult, that the joy and fulfillment he derives from the secret knowledge (never mind that it is not knowledge) of his flat-Earth cult is nothing more or less than the *makarismos* enjoyed by initiates into the ancient mysteries. It is all around him: A young mother says that she wishes the people she loves "could feel what I feel" when she meditates upon the truth of the flatness of the Earth.

Everybody is after that feeling: the flat-Earthers, the QAnon dopes who have got themselves so torqued up that the feebs are worried about them as a terrorism threat, the Bernie Sanders partisans whispering darkly about the "rigged" economy and the shadowy billionaires acting behind the scenes who control the media, the corporations, the government. . . . The social exclusion and isolation that comes from joining a mystery cult isn't a terrible price to pay but one of the main benefits, the mechanism by which the cult imbues its members with a sense of new identity. They speak about flat-Earth belief as something that follows a conversion experience and sadly note the apostasy of one high-profile social-media advocate who recently left their community.

Which is to say: One conspiracy theory is very like another. The people out in the pews are in a cult, but the men on the stage and hawking books and DVDs and such do not have the faces and souls and elocutions of cult leaders—no, they are exactly like the guys who want to sell you a vacation timeshare in Belize, "official" President Donald J. Trump memorial gold coins, miracle cures for baldness or fatness or arthritis or diabetes. And they know what their product is. It isn't geography lessons.

"His name was 'Adolf,'" says an older man standing in the lobby. "He was the first politician to figure out the lie." (Spoiler alert: Yes, he meant *that* Adolf.) In front of him is a small knot of dumpy flushed anxious Tammys with forearm tattoos, pale wan broken men in Australian bush hats, older guys in denim overalls, and younger men with beards and beanie hats, trying to figure out how to get five dollars off their Embassy Suites Hotel Convention Center and Spa parking bill, scanning their tickets and punching buttons on a machine with a label offering in big seventy-two-point type: VALIDATION.

Pillars of Fire

Midland-Odessa, Texas

THIS PLACE IS KNOWN FOR TWO THINGS: One of them is what locals lovingly refer to as THAT GODDAMNED BOOK, and the other one is oil—the oil business, oil money, and oil jobs, none of which is ever very far from the minds of the good citizens here, from shift laborers to the degreed-up nerds of VERY HIGH TECH to the inevitable rash of bankers and lawyers who crop up like mushrooms wherever money is being made, even under the pitiless glare of Buzz Bissinger's "Friday-night lights," even when all of Midland, Texas, is gathered in prayer to the ONE TRUE GOD WHO ABIDETH IN THE END ZONE, even when it's crosstown rivals facing off, the Midland Bulldogs against the Robert E. Lee Rebels—Robert E. Lee High School being the alma mater of Laura Bush, Tommy Lee Jones, Rex and Ryan Tucker, and Junior Miller—even when the home-team quarterback, a 6′4″ 221-pound beast of a high-school kid who rejoices in the superhero-worthy name of "Suddin Sapien," crashes over the Rebels like Sherman to sneak a keeper across the goal line.

In truth, Sapien & Co. are having a rough time of it tonight. The Rebels have a couple of big mean guys in the backfield who spend the game manhandling the defensive linemen who are supposed to be manhandling them: The Rebels run the ball about seventy yards up the middle for a touchdown on their second play, which does nothing at all for the spirits of the home team. It doesn't get any better for the Bulldogs. As the first quarter comes to a close, the young Bulldog sitting behind me tells her grandmother that her frustration is so intense that she's going to have to switch to Spanish for the remainder of the evening. The couple down front in T-shirts identifying them as the parents of a mixed family—"Two Rebels, One Bulldog"—try not to act more than one-third excited. Sapien puts up a manful fight with a high-stakes long-range passing game, but in the end the Rebels literally run away with it.

If it isn't much of a game, the spectacle is something: The Bulldogs' purple-plumed marching band covers the entire field, and there are ranks and ranks of cheerleaders—they seem to have about four different kinds, each class in distinct livery—and the home team takes the field barreling out of the mouth of a giant inflatable bulldog. The visiting Rebels—they're *technically* the visitors tonight, though the two teams in fact share the stadium, which has a capacity of eighteen thousand people—come out through a much less impressive inflatable arch, but they have a smoke machine, which buys some cool points. There's all sorts of Two Americas cultural distinctiveness on display here, the sort of thing that gives the willies to your familiar irony-dipped secular-urban Brooklyn-dwelling M.F.A. types, from the evangelical hand-holding among team captains as they stride out onto the field to the weird little military ceremony that has for some reason become a standard part of the order of gridiron worship, and, Cupcake, you'd better *believe* that all hats come off of all heads when the high-school ROTC honor guard comes out to present Old Glory, even the band trumpeters who step forward to play a fanfare set their tall shakos down on the artificial turf, and nobody but nobody is taking a knee.

It's an impressive display and, one cannot help but calculate, an expensive one, especially in a county that pretty seriously considered shutting down its public libraries not too long ago. But it's no mystery where the money comes from—it's on billboards all around the stadium:

RK Pump and Supply, Henry Resources, Concho: "Midland-Based and Midland Proud," Anadarko, Occidental Petroleum. Out there in the stands, the line between fleece-vested Wall Street finance bro and fleece-vested Midland petro bro is not entirely distinct, and that is no accident. The oil-and-gas business out here accounts for only 20 percent of direct employment, but those 20 percent of workers account for 70 percent of wages. A young roustabout who cheerfully describes his job as "mixing mud!"—preparing fracking fluids—also cheerfully reports that he'll make about $90,000 this year. He's twenty-one years old. And, of course, a great many of the workers not directly employed in energy-related concerns are effectively auxiliaries to the industry, from restaurant owners to Uber drivers.

A few lucky kids from this little island of civilization in the desolate and blasted Martian landscape of West Texas have gone on to make their fortunes in football and other sports. One of them, Susan Graham, became a famous opera star. But there are a lot more fortunes to be made out there in the mud, mixing it up.

"THIS TOWN USED TO HAVE A ROLLS-ROYCE DEALERSHIP," says Stephen Robertson of the Permian Basin Petroleum Association. "That was back in the sixties, when Midland probably had sixty thousand residents." Things have changed a little since then: You see the occasional Range Rover and a fair number of Rolexes, but the billboards mainly advertise the latest in fashion that is "FR"—flame resistant. Dangerous business, oil and gas.

Midland's population is a tale of boom and stagnation, though mostly boom: It went from 9,352 in the 1940 census to 21,713 in 1950 before nearly trebling to 62,625 in 1960. In 1970, it fell back below 60,000. Then came the 1970s oil crisis, which saw Midland's population jump up to 70,525 in 1980 and 89,443 in 1990. High oil prices aren't a "crisis" around here: They are manna from heaven. The population of Midland currently sits at 136,089 permanent residents, though it also has a substantial itinerant workforce, many of them housed in the semi-permanent "man camps" that have cropped up around the oil patch in response to the city's chronic housing shortage. The median rent on an apartment in Midland is almost three times what it is in comparable nearby Texas cities—closer to Southern California than to most of West Texas. Midland's slightly more rough-and-tumble sister city, Odessa—"the worst town on earth," Larry McMurtry called it in *Texasville*—is not a lot more affordable.

There is a great deal of highly specialized short-term work in the oil business, with crews traveling from place to place as needed. One of the results of this is that Midland has a kind of upside-down hotel market, in which weeknight rentals are about 2.5 times the weekend rate. Investors and bankers with a lot of history in the cyclical (sometimes viciously cyclical) oil business are hesitant to put a lot of money into construction of apartment buildings and lower-cost developments, so houses out here tend to be built one at a time. There are vacant and underused buildings downtown ripe for residential conversion, but the high up-front costs (asbestos abatement is a factor in many old buildings) have discouraged the sort of developers who might have jumped feet first into another booming market. The geologists and engineers and pipeline builders are confident that they can find the oil, but they sometimes have a hard time finding the workers.

"One of our issues is workforce growth," Robertson says. He is a lawyer by profession, but he has spent many years in and around the oil business and takes a clear-eyed view of its ups and downs. "We have a product and a price that responds to supply and demand, and that's the reality. Things can change." One of the problems the industry faces during booms is that people act like they will never end. "How do you take a kid who is in high school, who maybe comes from a one-parent family where that parent is making $90,000 a year driving a truck, and convince him that that's not what he should do after high school—or even during high school? How do you convince him to stay on and continue with his education? We need engineers, we need geologists, we need these highly technical jobs. You might make $70,000 . . . *this* year. But you'll make so much more if you pursue your education."

But that doesn't necessarily mean a four-year degree. The oil business has a little bit of a gap in the middle of the education curve: They know where to get low-skilled labor, and they know where to get engineers and guys with Ph.D.s. But there's a blue-collar sweet spot in between for skilled tradesmen, from welders to pipefitters. The local school system has set up something called the "Petroleum Academy," which supports the educational development of both college-bound students and those interested in oil-field jobs that require some further education but something short of a bachelor's degree in engineering. And once those workers are in oil-field jobs, there is real value to continuing education oriented toward professional development rather than toward an academic degree.

The invisible hand of the local labor market is pretty efficient at connecting low-skilled workers with low-skilled oil-field jobs, some of which pay pretty well, and most of which pay a lot better than the next-best job a low-skilled worker is likely to find. But a little extra something can make a huge difference: The local Chick-fil-A is offering thirteen dollars an hour to start, which is not bad for a fast-food job that guarantees you Sundays off, but a guy with a class-A commercial driver's license—or a guy with a clean driving record who can *get* a class-A CDL—might plausibly pocket a signing bonus that amounts to most of what that thirteen-dollar-an-hour food-service worker would earn in a year.

(An interesting cultural consequence of the local labor market: Those oil-field jobs are largely though by no means exclusively held by men, and the daytime work of the city's service industries, from restaurants to hotels, appears to be done almost exclusively by women. I did not encounter a single man working a customer service job during daylight hours, though some younger, student-age men showed up at those jobs in the evenings.)

"The American dream of being able to pull yourself up by your bootstraps—that's what the oil business offers," Robertson says. Lots of people move to Midland for white-collar jobs—you can overhear them talking biocides over cigars and fine wine on the patio of the Hemingway as Ford F-350 Super Duty trucks idle in the lot looking for a parking space—but fewer workers make their way to the oil patch for blue-collar jobs, even the high-paying ones on offer in Midland.

Why not?

"Where would you put them?" Robertson asks. "Think about the man camps—it's right there in the name: It's not a place you bring your family."

WHEN PEOPLE THINK OF OIL, they think of Exxon, Chevron, Shell— "Big Oil," as they are sometimes denounced. But that's not really quite right. Petroleum economist Karr Ingham calculates that, in Texas, independent operators drill 96 percent of the wells and produce 92 percent of the oil. For years, many of the majors acted essentially as landlords, holding leases and taking their royalties but leaving the hard and dirty work—and the big investments—to others.

That has started to change because of developments both technological and political.

The Permian Basin was, for many years, consigned to the ash heap of "legacy" production, meaning that the conventional wisdom was that the reserves had been identified, the wells had been drilled, and all that was left to do was to keep those wells operating until they went dry. That would be that for the Permian Basin, and for Midland. But the combination of hydraulic fracturing and horizontal drilling undid that conventional wisdom, unlocking a Saudi Arabia's worth of oil and gas in Texas and New Mexico and more elsewhere throughout the United States and North America. The Permian Basin went from producing about 1 million barrels of oil a day to producing 3.5 million, and within a few years it is expected to produce 7 million. The pressing problem right now isn't getting at the oil but getting that oil to market, as production threatens to exceed pipeline capacity. Industry leaders are confident that transportation will keep up with production; the real challenges, in the eyes of many of them, are related to public goods, governance, and quality-of-life issues: making sure that the communities in which they operate have good schools and enough of them, doctors and hospitals, and roads.

Seven million barrels a day: That would be a lot of oil. But it's complicated: In spite of what the politicians sometimes say, the United States is not a net exporter of oil; the country's net imports of oil run on average from 2.5 million to 3 million barrels a day, according to the U.S. Energy Information Administration, though the same agency forecasts that 2018's net imports will be about 60 percent less than those in 2017, with the United States importing the smallest share of its oil since the 1950s.

The problem is that oil is not an undifferentiated commodity: There's light oil, which is what the United States mostly produces, and there's heavy oil, which accounts for about 90 percent of the crude the United States imports. Because the United States was for so long oriented toward imported heavy oil, most U.S. refineries are optimized for that kind of crude. In fact, the United States does not have the refining capacity to process all the oil known as "Texas light sweet" coming out of the Permian Basin—which is why the federal government's recent decision to lift its insane ban on oil exports has been so important to the players in Midland: They had the oil, but they needed a market. If you are looking for a free-trade success story, come to Midland.[1]

That has emboldened the oil industry. It also has emboldened the United States government, which just moved to reimpose all of the sanctions on Tehran that had been lifted by the Obama administration. Thirty years ago, the prospect of the Iranians' getting froggy and shutting down the Strait of Hormuz was enough to clench sphincters from the Oval Office to Downing Street. And oil prices are determined in a very dynamic worldwide market, meaning that Middle Eastern shenanigans still have the capacity to punch Americans in the wallet. But the United States is also on its way toward becoming the world's largest oil exporter—and, as of September 2017, the United States was the world's largest *producer* of crude oil. If the ayatollahs get wild, things might not go the way they did the last time around. The most likely outcome would be the reopening of that Rolls-Royce dealership in Midland. A senior executive says that he expects the coming few years to be "transformative" not only for the oil business but also for everything it touches, from the domestic economy to foreign policy.

We have the oil, and we have the technique for getting to it. What's needed is physical infrastructure. Between 1998 and 2014, there was not a single new refinery built in the United States. At the beginning of 2018, five new ones had come online, one in South Dakota and the rest in Texas. The Port of Corpus Christi is now the nation's largest oil-export facility, and it is developing at a staggering pace: Geneva-based commodities trader Trafigura recently put $1 billion into an export terminal in Corpus Christi, allowing it to service Suezmax tankers, the big boys that can hold 1 million barrels of crude. Now the same firm is planning to fund an offshore buoy to service VLCCs—Very Large Crude Carriers—the truly gigantic oil transporters that can bear 2 million barrels of crude at a time, which are too large to squeeze comfortably into existing infrastructure. That's another few hundred million dollars in investment in real physical capital. The next time somebody tries to tell you that "financialization" has led to "deindustrialization," give that some thought.

None of this is pretty. There's no such thing as clean energy. Oil, gas, nuclear, the endless colonies of wind turbines looming over the Texas prairie—even the great green god of solar power must bow to that reality: Do you know what the panels that photovoltaic cells are mounted in are made of? They are made of polyester. Do you know what polyester is made of? It is made of oil. Natural gas may burn cleaner than coal, but getting to it can be ugly. Energy is about trade-offs, and the oil business employs more professional environmentalists than probably any other business in the world. You would not believe how much investment—and professional peer pressure—has gone into making sure that Permian Basin oil production does not unduly disturb the lesser prairie chicken and the dunes sagebrush lizard. The oil industry tends to go above and beyond what's legally required of it as a way of keeping the EPA at least a little bit at bay. But there are all sorts of challenges, from earthquakes to the more mundane (but probably more consequential) business of dealing with fracking wastewater. Managing those is a full-time job for a lot of very bright and earnest people with expensive educations and mandates from the public and private sectors both. Almost to a man and woman, they inspire confidence.

I am a native of this place, and I have a great deal of affection for it, but not so much as to fail to appreciate that Providence has located much of this country's oil where getting at it would do the least violence to the natural pulchritude of the American landscape. You could build thirty refineries and five New York Cities between Midland and Dallas without disturbing much of anybody besides a few rattlesnakes and perhaps the good people of Sweetwater, Texas, whose annual Rattlesnake Roundup is the social event of the season. (Congratulations to Cyera Pieper, winner of this year's Miss Snake Charmer pageant.) But all in all, one naturally prefers a world in which the lesser prairie chicken may frolic freely across the desert, fulfilling his natural role in the local ecosystem: coyote chow.

The first European to venture into these parts was Francisco Vázquez de Coronado y Luján, who reported in 1541: "I reached some plains so vast that I did not find their limit anywhere I went, although I traveled over them for more than 300 leagues. With no more landmarks than if we had been swallowed up by the sea . . . there was not a stone, nor bit of rising ground, nor a tree, nor a shrub, nor anything to go by." The explorer had his men drive wooden stakes into the ground at regular intervals, a makeshift trail of breadcrumbs to lead them home out of that big, vast, empty place. Hence the region is known to this day as the "Llano Estacado," the staked plain. It is not quite so featureless now: The black towers of oil refineries rise like sinister citadels out of the desert, along with the truck stops, the billboards, and, closer to town, the churches and massage parlors that both tend to abound in oil-patch towns.

And then there are the flare stacks, the great tall towers used to vent unusable waste gas out of oil and gas wells, which send dramatic columns of fire up into the night sky: pillars of fire, which ought really to resonate in the imaginations of these largely churchgoing communities but which are passed by as though they were no more remarkable than a bus stop or another franchise casual-dining restaurant. The new breed of investors and producers may be in it for the long term, but there still is a feeling of *temporariness* around much of the oil industry—all those cheap steel buildings and portable man-camp trailer huts under these tall skies, clinging to what is obviously comprehensible as the thin and rocky crust of a planet. Driving across it, you get the feeling that one good biblical storm could wipe this whole slate clean, that there would be nothing left behind except the utility poles, which look like they've been there forever, stakes on the plain left by a different breed of explorers after a different kind of gold.

In the Valley of the Giant Robots

Canonsburg, Pennsylvania

IN THE MIDDLE-OF-FRACKIN'-NOWHERE PENNSYLVANIA, Boy Genius is showing off his giant robot: It's about 150 feet tall, God and the almighty engineers alone know how many hundreds of tons of steel, and four big, flat duck feet on bright orange legs. "Yeah, this is kind of cool," he says of his supersized Erector Set project. "You can set those feet at 45 degrees, and it will walk around in circles all day," a colleague adds.

But Boy Genius is not letting himself get too excited about all this—it's pretty clearly not his first giant robot, and he's a lot more excited about his seismic-imaging system: "It's kind of like a GPS, but it's underground and it works with the Earth's magnetic characteristics." Nods all around—that *is* cool. Everybody here has a three-day beard and a hard hat and steel-toed work boots, but there's a strong whiff of chess club and Science Olympiad in the air, young men who are no strangers to the pocket protector, who in adolescence discovered an unusual facility for fluid dynamics, and who are now beavering away at mind-clutchingly complex technical problems, one of which is how to get a 150-foot-tall tower of machinery from A to B without taking it apart and trucking it (solution: add duck feet). The giant robot may walk, but it isn't too fast: It can take half a day to move twenty feet, because this isn't a *Transformers* movie, this is THE

181

PLAY, and Boy Genius is a member of the startlingly youthful and bespectacled tribe of engineers swarming out of the University of Pittsburgh and the Colorado School of Mines and Penn State and into the booming gas fields of Pennsylvania, where the math weenies are running the show in the Marcellus Shale, figuring out how to suck a Saudi Arabia's worth of natural gas out of a vein of hot and impermeable rock thousands of feet beneath the green valleys of Penn's woods. Forget about your wildcatters, your roughnecks, your swaggering Texans in big hats: The nerds have taken over.

The weird little in-house argot of gas exploration has more plays than Stephen Sondheim: the conventional-gas play, the shallow-gas play, the Gothic play, the Wyoming play, and the gold-plated godfather of them all, the Marcellus play, which stretches from West Virginia to New York and contains hundreds of trillions of cubic feet of natural gas. Exactly how much is recoverable is a matter of hot dispute, but the general consensus is: a whole bunch, staggering amounts quantified in numbers that have to be written in exponential expressions (maybe it's 1.7×10^{14} cubic feet, maybe 4.359×10^{14}), with the estimates on the higher end suggesting the equivalent of fifteen years of total U.S. energy use. There's so much efficiently combustible stuff down there that the boy geniuses have to spend hours in esoteric preparations for what to do about the oil and gas they hit that they don't mean to—they're after the Marcellus gas, but there's a lot of other methane on the way down.

Given that oil imports account for about half of the total U.S. trade deficit, that U.S. policymakers suffer from debilitating insomnia every time some random ayatollah starts making scary noises about the Strait of Hormuz, and that about half of American electricity comes from burning coal—which, on its very best day, is a lot more environmentally problematic than natural gas (something to think about while tooling down to Trader Joe's in your 45 percent coal-powered Chevy Volt or Nissan Leaf)—exploiting natural gas to its full capability has the potential to radically alter some fundamental economic, national-security, and environmental equations of keen interest in these overextended and

underemployed United States. Tens of thousands of new jobs already
have been created (Want $60,000 a year and a $2,000 signing bonus to
drive a water truck? Pennsylvania is calling!), and tens of billions of dollars in new wealth has been injected into the ailing U.S. economy since
Marcellus production really picked up around 2008. Pennsylvania and
West Virginia saw 57,000 new Marcellus jobs in a single year, as firms
ranging from scrappy independents to giants such as Royal Dutch Shell
poured billions of dollars into shale investments—land, equipment,
buildings, roads, machinery: capital, in a word. Massive capital.

Cheap, relatively clean, ayatollah-free energy, enormous investments
in real capital and infrastructure, thousands of new jobs for blue-collar
workers and Ph.D.s alike, Americans engineering something other than
financial derivatives—who couldn't love all that?

Josh, mostly.

Everybody in the Marcellus play is on a first-name basis with Josh
Fox, even though few of them have met the young director who with a
single fraudulent image in his documentary *Gasland*—footage of a
Colorado man turning on his kitchen sink and setting the tap water on
fire—brought into existence a new crusade for the Occupy Whatever set
and a new Public Enemy No. 1 for the Luddite Left: gas exploration,
specifically the extraction technique of hydraulic fracturing, popularly
known as "fracking."

FRACKING WORKS LIKE THIS: You set up your giant robot and you
drill a five-inch-diameter hole down several thousand feet until you hit
the gas shale, and then you turn ninety degrees and you drill horizontally
through some more shale, until you've got all your pipes and rig in place.
And then you hit that shale with a high-pressure blast of water and sand,
creating millimeter-wide fractures through which the natural gas can
escape and make you very, very rich in spite of the fact that you're spending about a million dollars a week on space-age "matrix" drill bits and
squadrons of engineers and a small army of laborers, technicians, truck
drivers, machinists, and a pretty-good-sized bill from Hogfather's, the

local barbecue joint that has added a couple of specialized and custom-outfitted mobile crews just for cooking two massive meals a day for the fracking hands who are far too busy to take off for lunch. (Sure, Exxon-Mobil is going to be making a killing, but fracking's biggest boosters may be the local restaurateurs who are cooking with gas while cooking for gas, and are happy to serve workers straight from the field: "No Mud on the Floor, No Cash in the Drawer" says the sign in a local diner.) The water makes the fractures, and the sand keeps them open. There's some other stuff in that fracking blend, too: biocides, for one thing, not very different from the chlorine in your swimming pool, to keep bacteria and algae and other gunk from growing in the water and clogging up the works. There are also some friction reducers, because water and sand moving at speed can produce a lot of wear and tear (see the Grand Canyon), and the occasional jolt of 7 percent hydrochloric acid solution for boring out holes in the concrete. The mix is 99+ percent water and sand, and the rest of the stuff is mostly run-of-the-mill industrial chemicals (those friction reducers use a polymer that also is used in children's toys, for example). Real concerns, but not exactly an insurmountable environmental challenge.

Not only is this happening more than a mile beneath the surface, it's also happening at a level that is separated from the closest points of the aquifer by a layer of impermeable rock three or four or five Empire State Buildings deep. "We couldn't frack through that if we were *trying* to," says one engineer working the Marcellus. "The idea that we could do so by accident is crazy. Not while we're fracking with water and sand. Nukes, maybe, but not water and sand."

So what about that burning water?

The weird true thing is that water has been catching fire for a long time—"a long time" here meaning way back into the mists of obscure prehistory and the realm of legend. The temple of the Oracle of Delphi was built on the site of a burning spring said to have been discovered by a bewildered goatherd around 1000 B.C., and sundry antique heathens across the Near East had rituals related to burning bodies of water. The geographically minded among you will appreciate that there are several places in the United States named "Burning Springs," including prominent ones in such energy-intensive locales as Kentucky and West Virginia. There's a Burning Springs in New York, too, and seventeenth-century missionaries wrote in awe about Indians' setting fire to the waters of Lake Erie and nearby streams. Water wells were catching fire in Pennsylvania as early as the eighteenth century, well before anybody was fracking for gas.

You wouldn't know it from watching *Gasland*, but that Colorado community made famous by the film has had water catching on fire since at least the 1930s, and the Colorado Division of Water chronicled "troublesome amounts of . . . methane" in the water back in 1976. As it turns out, places that have a lot of gas in the ground *have a lot of gas in the ground*. And sometimes that gas is in the water, too, as the result of natural geological processes.

Which isn't to say that gas drilling can't muck up drinking-water wells. That can and does happen—but it has nothing to do with fracking. If anything, fracking is less likely to pollute groundwater than are other forms of drilling, because it happens so far from the water, with so much rock in between, which isn't the case with shallower wells and more traditional forms of gas exploration.

"METHANE MIGRATION IS REAL," says John Hanger, an environmental activist in Pennsylvania who served as head of the state's department of environmental protection under the liberal governorship of Democrat Ed Rendell. "Prior to the Marcellus, there have probably been 50 to 150 private water wells, out of more than a million in the state, that have had methane contamination as a result of mistakes in the drilling process—but that has nothing to do with fracking. Some in the industry deny that it ever happens, and that is false. But frack fluids returning from depth, from 5,000 to 8,000 feet under the ground, to contaminate an aquifer? When the industry says that's never happened, that has in fact *never happened*."

Colorado's gas regulator took the unusual step of releasing a public debunking of *Gasland*'s claim that fracking is responsible for that flaming faucet. Confronted with the facts—call them "an inconvenient truth"—Fox responded that they were "not relevant." But what is not relevant is that image of a burning water faucet, at least if you want to understand the facts about fracking, which the anti-frack fanatics don't.

The problem with fracking mostly isn't what goes down the pipe, but what comes up, and the real hairy environmental challenge turns out to be the relatively un-sexy matter of wastewater management. Gas drillers put their bits down through a lot of ancient seabeds, meaning that the water comes up saturated with our tasty friend NaCl, also known as salt. Given that a great many examples of aquatic and riparian flora and fauna are evolved to do well in fresh water but curl up and die in salt water—especially salt water that's considerably saltier than the saltiest seawater—you can't just dump that stuff in the Susquehanna River. And then there's potassium salts and such. And then there's other stuff that comes up, too, substances you'd just as soon see remain buried in the depths of the earth: arsenic, for one thing, and the darkly-whispered-about entity known in drilling circles as NORM—Naturally Occurring Radioactive Material—and various other kinds of VERY BAD STUFF. Of particular concern is the presence of bromides, which, when combined with the chlorine used in water-treatment facilities, have a worrisome tendency to turn into the Seal Team Six of volatile organic compounds, basically a big flashing neon sign reading "CANCER."

There are other workaday environmental problems endemic to fracking: For the three to five days a frack lasts, it's loud—really, really loud, because it's basically a construction site, with a vast array of pumps and compressors and giant margarita mixers blending sand into the water, and a big battery of generators to run it all. There's not much to be done about the noise, though you're typically not fracking real close to densely populated areas. A few firms have hit upon the novel approach of simply offering nearby homeowners money to go away for the week, expenses paid, or at least putting them up in a hotel for the duration. (An idled fracking rig might cost you $1 million a week—you can afford to pay a lot of HoJo bills to keep that from happening.) The trucks cause traffic snarls, so they're building more pipelines to replace the trucks, but digging pipelines can be an inconvenience, too. Fracking for gas is not zero-impact. There's no easy way around that.

And there's certainly no easy way around the water issues, either. Disposing of wastewater is a challenge from all sides: PR, technical, environmental, and economic. But a number of the drillers have come up with a nearly ideal solution for disposing of it: Don't.

A couple of hundred miles away from Boy Genius and his giant robot, in the Marcellus heartland of Williamsport, Pennsylvania, is TerrAqua Resource Management, one of the many private firms that have sprung up throughout THE PLAY to do what the local wastewater-treatment plants and municipal authorities aren't equipped to do and probably shouldn't be expected to do: treat nasty drilling water so that it can be used again. Trucks pull up, unload their murky liquid cargo, and then fill up on usable water to take back to the next job. Inside, a trio of vast water tanks, chemical vats, some sand filters, and a bunch more engineers make that water reusable. The facility has been up and running for only a couple of years, but millions of gallons of water already have passed through it. The solids get filtered out and disposed of, bacteria get biocided, and everybody makes the department of environmental protection happy by providing a government-certified "beneficial reuse" of drilling water.

Interesting thing: The place doesn't stink. It's got a slightly earthy smell to it, like the nursery section at Home Depot, but it doesn't smell like you'd expect a water-treatment plant to smell.

TerrAqua makes its living from the dirty end of the gas business, and its executives are under no illusions about the industry. There are good eggs—or at least self-interested, large-cap eggs who appreciate how much they have to lose if they get sloppy—and then there are what the locals call the "gassholes," by which they do not mean to denote the channel down which the pipe goes.

"There's *compliance*, and there's *high* compliance," says TerrAqua vice president Marty Muggleton. "There are companies that like to have a lot of extra cushion between where they are and where they have to be, and then there are those who like to get their toes close to the edge. And I think the industry has figured out which one of those you really want to be."

THE ONE YOU WANT TO BE, everybody from environmental activists to industry insiders says, is a company like Range Resources, a Texas-based firm that owns a big part of THE PLAY south of Pittsburgh, operating out of the hamlet of Canonsburg, Pennsylvania, near the West Virginia border. Like practically everybody else in town, they have a bunch of shiny new space in a corporate park that was barely half-populated until the Marcellus began to get going. It's a busy anthill with a lot of boots and surprisingly few suits. Range is one of the companies that have figured out that there's so much money coming out of the shale—even with gas down near two dollars—that it pays to go above and beyond. Their trucks tear up the roads in Canonsburg, so they build newer and better roads than the ones they found, spending more money on roads than the city itself does. There are a surprising number of speed traps around town, but they aren't the local Barney Fifes: They're contractors hired by Range keeping an eye on the company's drivers, who get fired for speeding or otherwise behaving in a gassholish fashion. The old days of what they call "Texas-style" gas development are mostly past: The billion-dollar boys have a lot of resources to throw at environmental problems and a lot to lose.

"Pennsylvania used to have surface disposal," says Range's Matt Pitzarella, "and West Virginia still does. That's just crazy." "Surface disposal" means "just dumping it in the river or on the ground." Pennsylvania, he points out, has a long history of environmental grief related to the energy industry, from acidic mine discharges to thousands of forgotten (and not always well-capped) oil wells dating from back in the days of Colonel Drake, the genius who noticed that farmers drilling water wells kept hitting oil and figured he might as well drill for the oil. Thousands of steel casings were ripped out of wells during World War II, and thousands of miles of waterways in the state have been befouled, mostly by mine discharges. Natural gas is pretty clean at the combustion point, and Range wants to be the firm that shows how clean it can be during the preceding stages. "If anything, the microscope that we as an industry are under has made us more innovative. Some of the tactics they use may be unfair. It's not fair to paint us all with the same broad brush. But at the same time, it's not fair for the industry to paint all the environmentalists with the same broad brush, either." Recycling water rather than discharging it has been a fundamental change for the industry's environmental impact and, as long as the water is cleaned up enough that it doesn't muck up the works, it's all the same to the drillers. "We could frack with peanut butter, if we had enough of it," Pitzarella says.

FRACKING WITH SKIPPY never occurred to George Mitchell, the legendary gasman who staked his fortune on the seemingly crackpot idea that you could efficiently get gas out of a rock, but he tried everything else. Range engineer Mark Whitley was with Mitchell in the early days, and still gets a little edge in his voice when he talks about the dicey prospect of having invested about $1 billion of a company worth only about that much in a technology that nobody thought would work. Noting that President Obama claimed that "it was public research dollars" that made shale extraction possible, he laughs without mirth, and looks like he wants to spit: "Not true," he says. "We tried everything known to man to get a rock to produce. There's a lot of people who claim to be the father of the Marcellus, but if you didn't put any money in or take any gas out, then what's that? It was industry studies, industry experience, and industry dollars that did this, and we've driven up production more rapidly than anybody thought possible." And it was far from a done deal for years: "We could have thrown in the towel any time during the first ten years, but the one guy who didn't want to quit was the guy in charge: George." (*George.* Not, incidentally, *Barack.*) They tried all sorts of brews to get the shale to give up the gas, and, as the expenses mounted, they tried cheaper and cheaper alternatives, eventually settling on the low-tech combination of water and sand that turned out to be the thing that actually works. "Economics drove it," Whitley says.

The gas guys scoff at President Obama's claim that federal ingenuity produced the shale boom, and they scoff harder at their rivals' occasional pleas for government handouts, notably T. Boone Pickens's plan to have the government require long-haul trucks to convert to natural gas and then have taxpayers pick up the bill for it.[1] "The best thing the federal government can do is stay out of our way," Whitley says. "Leave us alone, and we are happy. We are well and appropriately regulated by the state."

Practically everybody in the industry speaks well, if sometimes begrudgingly, of Pennsylvania's department of environmental protection, which, after being caught flat-footed in the early days of the shale revolution, has gotten with the program in a big way. The state has undergone a major overhaul of its regulatory regime, and by most measures Pennsylvania's gas industry is cleaner and safer today than in the pre-fracking era. Billions of dollars rolling in, and thousands of new jobs, and much more on the line in the future, will do that. And the industry, while not always entirely in love with the DEP and its colonoscopic minions, appreciates that its Pennsylvania regulators understand the practices and geology of Pennsylvania in a way that faraway regulators at the EPA would not. If the EPA—especially a highly politicized EPA under a Democratic administration—got involved, the result would likely have been arbitrary national standards. "The feds only screw things up," says one engineer, and any reasonable federal regulatory regime would end up essentially replicating most or all of what the states already are doing, but at a political distance that makes regulators more remote and less accountable. When it comes to fracking for gas, facts on the ground are facts literally in the ground. Keeping regulation at the state level is the top political priority in the Marcellus, so the industry has an interest in making the DEP look good: It's that compliance-versus-high-compliance thing again, naked self-interest producing virtuous outcomes. Range regularly has the DEP out to its facilities to show them the latest and greatest, with the unspoken suggestion that what it does voluntarily everybody else in THE PLAY should do voluntarily, too, because voluntarily accepted best practices are the only real political insurance against involuntarily accepted second-best (or worse) practices: *Let's do it right before the feds make us do it wrong.*

DEP spokesman Kevin Sunday encourages that line of thinking: "Pennsylvania has a unique and diverse geology, and that's why states should have the primacy in regulating this instead of the one-size-fits-all approach that some in the federal government would prefer to see." He says that water recycling has represented a "sea change" in the industry. "Some are recycling at 100 percent—it depends on what you're drilling through. The average is 70, 75 percent." Higher standards for discharged water have made it more attractive to recycle, too, with many facilities required to treat water to the state's standard for potable drinking water before putting it into streams or rivers. That's a sneaky little trick: Once the water has been cleaned up enough to discharge, nobody wants to discharge it. "If you get it down to that standard, it's too valuable to flush it down the toilet," Sunday says.

Which is to say that in the Marcellus they have discovered, along with enormous quantities of gas, that rarest of commodities: a regulatory success story.

"THERE IS NO DOUBT that drilling wastewater is highly polluted," says Hanger, the former DEP secretary. "Prior to the Marcellus, when the Pennsylvania industry was small, we were dumping drilling wastewater untreated into rivers and streams and hoping that dilution would keep concentrations below levels that would cause damage to aquatic life or drinking water. There is probably less water going untreated into the rivers today than before the first Marcellus well. It's a success story. If you look at the top ten things impacting water in Pennsylvania right now, the gas industry would not be on the list, and certainly not fracking. Industry, environmentalists, and regulators all ought to be celebrating. But there's money to be made out of fighting."

All of which is perplexing to the boy geniuses in the fracking command centers scattered around Pennsylvania. Talking politics with engineers is dancing about architecture—they just don't get it, and they get frustrated. "We have all this wealth in the ground," says one of the bespectacled brethren, "and we can get it out. We can do it efficiently and cleanly"—*and we have giant frackin' robots!*—"but some people don't want us to. They just don't like it." He wears a look that is four parts nonplussed and one part hurt. You want to hand the kid an Ayn Rand novel with the good parts dog-eared.

Nothing happens in a vacuum, political or environmental, even a mile under the rock. And the real question about fracking, as Hanger points out, isn't fracking versus some Platonic energy ideal. It's between fracking and coal, or, to a lesser extent, between fracking and oil.

Walking around finished gas wells in THE PLAY, you'll notice a weird thing: A lot of those gas wells run off of solar power. There's no utility connection in some of the more remote areas, and it's more efficient to put up some solar panels to run the monitoring equipment and the other gear necessary to keep a producing well producing. And in the remote Texas panhandle, Valero operates a major oil refinery that's attached to a 5,000-acre wind farm, being located in the sweet spot of having lots of crude pipelines, lots of wind, lots of real estate, and not very many people. When it's operating at its peak, the wind farm produces enough juice to run the whole refinery—but it takes a lot of turbines and a lot of West Texas wind to get that done when you have the capacity to refine 170,000 barrels of crude a day. The wind farm isn't a PR stunt, Valero insists: It's economical, and beyond wind, Valero has a pretty good-sized portfolio of investments in alternative energy, from ethanol to algae. But consumers and policymakers should understand the limitations of those technologies, a Valero spokesman says: "We get frustrated by this idea that cars should run on sunshine and happy thoughts." But cars can and do run on natural gas, and the surge in U.S. oil and gas production has made American firms more competitive with their overseas rivals and has led to a renaissance among local refineries.

Given all that, the data are on the side of fracking. But the political momentum is on the other side. It remains likely that the EPA will take its heavy hand to the industry, a development for which the enviro-Left, led by Occupy Wall Street, is positively howling, which is frustrating for environmentalists such as John Hanger. "If there's no fracking, the unavoidable consequence would be a sharp increase in oil and coal consumption. Even if environmental and public-health issues were your only concerns—leave aside national security and the economic impacts—that fact alone should give you some pause."

But don't bother with *evidence*: The opposition to fracking isn't at its heart environmental or economic or scientific. It's ideological, and that ideology is *nihilism*. Environmentalism is a movement that began with the fire on the Cuyahoga River in 1969 and a few brief years later had mutated into the Voluntary Human Extinction Movement (motto: "May we live long and die out!"), which maintains: "Phasing out the human race by voluntarily ceasing to breed will allow Earth's biosphere to return to good health. Crowded conditions and resource shortages will improve as we become less dense." (Good luck with that "less dense" thing, geniuses.)

Benign environmentalists are opposed to pollution, as all sensible people are; malign environmentalists are opposed to energy and most of what it enables. Their enemy isn't drilling rigs and ethane crackers and engineers and their technological marvels: Their enemy is the kind of civilization that makes such feats and wonders possible, the fact that a smart guy with a big idea can make a hole in the ground and summon up power from the vasty deep. Their enemy is *us*. We can debate best drilling practices, appropriate emissions regulation, wastewater-disposal techniques—the engineering stuff—and even harebrained ideas like the Pickens plan.

But we can't really debate the course of modern technological civilization with people who are opposed to modern technological civilization per se, your mostly middle-class and expensively miseducated (and, forgive me for noticing, but your overwhelmingly *white*) types afflicted with the ennui of affluence, who suddenly take a fancy to the idea that life might be lived more authentically with a bone in one's nose and a trip to the neighborhood shaman—the shaman who might, if the spirits smile upon him, initiate you into the ancient mysteries of the burning spring.

The White Minstrel Show

New York, New York

ICE-T HAS NEVER RECEIVED AN ACADEMY AWARD, which makes sense, inasmuch as his movies have been for the most part crap. But you have to give the man credit as an actor: Along with other gangster rappers such as Ice Cube, he turned in such a convincing performance—amplifying negative stereotypes about black men and selling white people their own Reagan-era racial panic back to them in a highly stylized form—that people still, to this day, believe he was the guy he played on stage. One social-media critic accused him of hypocrisy for having recorded the infamous song "Cop Killer" before going on to a very lucrative career playing a police officer on television. Ice-T gave the man an honest answer: "It's both acting, homie."

Acting, indeed.

Pretty good acting, too, across the board in the rap world. Consider the strange evolution of Tupac Shakur, who went from a quiet, effeminate young man, a former acting and ballet student at the Baltimore School for the Arts apparently pointed like a rocket at a career in musical theater, to the "Thug Life" antihero persona that made him famous in a remarkably short period of time. He played tough guy Roland Bishop in *Juice* and basically stayed in character for the rest of his public life. As with Ice-T, many of his fans assumed the stage persona was the real man. There's a whole weird little racial dynamic in there waiting for some doctoral student to sort it out. Nobody expects Anthony Hopkins to eat a census worker.

A theater critic can't really begrudge a performer for making a living, and Ice-T put on a great show. I do wonder how much damage those performers did by reinforcing and glamorizing criminal stereotypes of black men. And I do mean that I *wonder*—I do not *know*. Maybe the act is more obvious if you are the sort of person who is being dramatized or caricatured. (I experience something like that when I hear modern country songs on the radio, all that cheerful alcoholism and casual adultery and ridiculous good ol' boy posturing.) It would be weird to describe black men as "acting black," but whatever they were up to was the opposite of "acting white."

There's a certain kind of conservative who loves to talk about "acting white"—that is, about the social sanction purportedly applied to African Americans who try too hard in school or who speak English that is too standard or who have interests and aspirations other than the ones that black people are stereotypically supposed to have. ("Acting white" isn't a complaint exclusive to African Americans. My friend Jay Nordlinger relates a wonderful story about the American Indian educator Ben Chavis, who was once accused by a sister of "acting white." His reply: "'Acting white' is not enough. I'm acting Jewish. Or maybe Chinese.") Oh, how we love to tut-tut knowingly about "acting white," implying that black Americans would be a good deal better off if they acted a little *more* white. That sort of thing is not entirely unique to conservatives, of course: Nine-tenths of all social criticism involving the problems of the American underclass consists of nice college graduates and policy professionals of many races and religions wondering aloud why *they* can't be more like *us*, which is why so much social policy is oriented toward trying to get more poor people to go to college, irrespective of whether they want to or believe they would benefit from going.

Conservatives have a weakness for that "acting white" business because, for rhetorical and political reasons that are too obvious to require much elaboration, we are intellectually invested in emphasizing the *self-inflicted* problems of black America. The "acting white" phenomenon may or may not be exaggerated. John McWhorter makes a pretty good case that it is a real problem. So did President Barack Obama, who called on the nation to "eradicate the slander that says a black youth with a book is acting white." I am not sure that a white man from Lubbock, Texas, has a great deal to add to President Obama's argument there.

But I do have something to say about the subject of white people acting white.

WE RARELY USED TO PUT IT IN RACIAL TERMS, unless we were talking about Eminem or the Cash-Me-Ousside Girl or some other white person who had embraced (or affected) some part of black popular culture. With the Trump-era emergence of a more self-conscious form of white-identity politics—especially white working-class identity politics—the racial language comes to the surface more often than it used to. But we still rarely hear complaints about "acting un-white." Instead, we hear complaints about "elitism."

The parallels to the "acting white" phenomenon in black culture are fairly obvious: When aspiration takes the form of explicit or implicit cultural identification, however partial, with some hated or resented outside group that occupies a notionally superior social position, then "authenticity" is to be found in socially regressive manners, mores, and habits. It is purely reactionary.

The results are quite strange. Republicans, once the party of the upwardly mobile with a remarkable reflex for comforting the comfortable, have written off entire sections of the country—including the bits where most of the people live—as "un-American." Silicon Valley and California at large, New York City and the hated Acela corridor, and to some extent large American cities categorically are sneered at and detested. There is some ordinary partisanship in that, inasmuch as the Democrats tend to dominate the big cities and the coastal metropolitan aggregations, but it isn't just that. Conservatives are cheering for the failure of California and slightly nonplussed that New York City still refuses to regress into being an unlivable hellhole in spite of the best efforts of its batty Sandinista mayor. Not long ago, to be a conservative on Manhattan's Upper East Side was the most ordinary thing in the world. Now that address would be a source of suspicion. God help you if you should ever attend a cocktail party in Georgetown, the favorite dumb trope of conservative talk-radio hosts.

We've gone from William F. Buckley Jr. to the gentlemen from *Duck Dynasty*. Why?

American authenticity, from the acting-even-whiter point of view, is not to be found in any of the great contemporary American business success stories, or in intellectual life, or in the great cultural institutions, but in the suburban-to-rural environs in which the white underclass largely makes its home—the world John Mellencamp sang about but understandably declined to live in.

Shake your head at rap music all you like: When's the last time you heard a popular country song about finishing up your master's in engineering at MIT?

White people acting white have embraced the ethic of the white *underclass*, which is distinct from the white *working* class, which has the distinguishing feature of regular gainful employment. The manners of the white underclass are Trump's—vulgar, aggressive, boastful, selfish, promiscuous, consumerist. The white *working* class has a very different ethic. Its members are, in the main, churchgoing, financially prudent, and married, and their manners are formal to the point of icy politeness. You'll recognize the style if you've ever been around it: It's "Yes, sir" and "No, ma'am," but it is the formality of soldiers and police officers—correct and polite, but not in the least bit deferential. It is a formality that does not acknowledge the superiority of social betters but rather asserts the equality of the speaker to any person or situation— perfectly *republican* manners. It is social respect rooted in genuine self-respect.

Its opposite is the sneering, leveling, drag-'em-all-down-into-the-mud anti-"elitism" of contemporary right-wing populism. Self-respect says: "I'm an American citizen, and I can walk into any room and talk to any president, prince, or potentate, because I can rise to any occasion." Populist anti-elitism says the opposite: "I can be rude enough and denigrating enough to drag anybody down to my level." Trump's rhetoric—ridiculous and demeaning schoolyard nicknames, boasting about money, and so forth—has always been about reducing. Trump doesn't have the intellectual capacity to duke it out with even the modest wits at the *New York Times*, hence it's "the failing *New York Times*."[1] Never mind that the *New York Times* isn't actually failing and that any number of Trump-related businesses have failed so thoroughly that they've gone into bankruptcy; the truth doesn't matter to the argument any more than it matters whether the fifth-grade bully actually has an actionable claim on some poor kid's lunch money. It would never even occur to the low-minded to identify with anybody other than the bully. That's what that ridiculous stuff about "winning" was all about in the campaign. It is might makes-right, the politics of chimpanzee troupes, prison yards, kindergartens, and other primitive environments. That is where the underclass ethic thrives—and how "smart people" came to be a term of abuse.

This inevitably involves a good deal of fakery.

The man at the center of all this atavistic redneck revanchism is a pampered billionaire real-estate heir from New York City, and it has been something to watch the multimillionaire populist pundits in Manhattan doing their best impersonations of beer-drinkin' regular guys from the sticks. I assume Sean Hannity picked up his purported love for country music in the sawdust-floored honky-tonks of . . . Long Island.

As a purely aesthetic enterprise, none of this clears my poor-white-trash cultural radar. I'm reminded of those so-called dive bars in Manhattan that spend $150,000 to make a pricey spot in Midtown look like a Brooklyn kid's idea of a low-rent roadside bar in Texas. (There's one that even has Lubbock license plates on the wall. I wonder where they got them—is there some kind of mail-order dive-bar starter kit that comes with taxidermy, Texas license plates, and a few cases of Lone Star? Maybe via Amazon Prime?)

The populist Right's abandonment of principle has been accompanied by a repudiation of good taste, achievement, education, refinement, and manners—all of which are abominated as signs of effete "elitism." During the Clinton years, Virtue Inc. was the top-performing share in the Republican political stock exchange. Fortunes were made, books were sold by the ton, and homilies were delivered. Today the same people are celebrating Donald Trump—not in spite of his being a dishonest, crude serial adulterer but because of it. His dishonesty, the quondam cardinals of Virtue Inc. assure us, is simply the mark of a savvy businessman, his vulgarity the badge of his genuineness and lack of "political correctness," and his pitiless abuse of his several wives and children the mark of a genuine "alpha male." No less a virtue entrepreneur than Bill Bennett dismissed those who pointed out Trump's endless lies and habitual betrayals as suffering from the "moral superiority" of people on "high horses," and said that Trump was simply "a guy who says some things awkwardly, indecorously, infelicitously."

Thus did the author of *The Book of Virtues* embrace the author of "Grab 'Em by the Pussy."

We need a Moynihan Report for conservative broadcasters.

The problem, in Bennett's telling (and that of many other conservatives), isn't that Trump is a morally defective reprobate but that he is aesthetically displeasing to overly refined "elitists." That is a pretty common line of argument—and an intellectual cop-out—but set that aside for the moment. Let's pretend that Bennett et al. are correct, and this is simply a matter of manners. Are we now to celebrate vulgarity as a virtue? Are we to embrace crassness? Are we supposed to pretend that a casino-cum-strip-joint is a civilizational contribution up there with Notre-Dame, that the Trump Taj Mahal trumps the Taj Mahal? Are we supposed to snigger at people who ask that question? Are we supposed to abandon our traditional defense of standards to mimic Trump's bucket-of-KFC-and-gold-plated-toilet routine?

Ludwig von Mises was as clear-eyed a social critic as he was an economist, and he noted something peculiar about the anti-Semitism of the Nazi era: In the past, minority groups had been despised for their purported vice—white American racists considered African Americans lazy and mentally deficient, the English thought the Irish drank too much to be trusted to rule their own country, everybody thought the Gypsies were put on this Earth to spread disease and thievery. But the Jews were hated by the Nazis for their *virtues*: They were too intelligent, too clever, too good at business, too cosmopolitan, too committed to their own distinctness, too rich, too influential, too thrifty.

Our billionaire-ensorcelled anti-elitists take much the same tack: Anybody with a prestigious job, a good income, an education at a selective university, and no oxy overdoses in the immediate family—and anybody who prefers hearing the New York Philharmonic at Lincoln Center to watching football on television—just doesn't know what life is like in "the real America." No, the "real America," in this telling, is little more than a series of dead factory towns, dying farms, pill mills—and, above all, *victims*. There, too, white people acting white echo elements of hip-hop culture, which presents powerful and violent icons of masculinity as hapless victims of American society.

The "alpha male" posturing, the valorizing of underclass dysfunction, the rejection of "elite" tastes and manners—right-wing populism in the age of Trump is a lot like Bruce Springsteen's act, once acidly (and perfectly) described as a "white minstrel show."

I wonder if Bill Bennett can tap-dance.

RACE IS PART OF THIS, as it is part of many things in America, but it is easy to make too much of it, too. The white underclass may suffer from "acting white," but what poor people in general suffer from is acting poor—repeating the mistakes and habits that have left them (or their parents and grandparents, in many cases) in poverty or near-poverty to begin with.

The more you know about that world, the less sympathetic you'll be to it. What the Trump-style would-be tribunes of the plebs have in common with self-appointed progressive advocates for the poor *is ignorance of the actual subject matter.* It weren't the scheming Chinaman what stole ol' Bubba's job down Bovina, 'cause ol' Bubba didn't really have him a job to steal. And it isn't capitalism that made rural Appalachia or small-town Texas what it is. Well-heeled children of privilege such as Elizabeth Bruenig condescend to speak on behalf of people about whom they know practically nothing—people who have not, let's remember, *asked* the well-scrubbed sons and daughters of the ruling class to speak on their behalf. When they *were* asked, they chose Donald Trump by a very large margin, but then the poor make poor choices all the time— that's part of why they're poor. The Left is convinced of Thomas Frank's *What's the Matter with Kansas?* thesis, that the poor and struggling in the conservative and rural parts of the country are just too besotted with Jesus talk and homosexual panic to understand what actually is at stake for them, and they therefore—the famous phrase—"vote against their own economic interests." Progressives preach about—and *to*—people with whom they have no real connection, and do so in ways that would embarrass them to death if it were a *racial* line rather than a *class* line they were crossing in such a state of pristine ignorance. They are the mirror image of white conservatives who wonder why poor black people in the Bronx can't just "act white" and get with the program.

If I might be permitted to address the would-be benefactors of the white underclass from the southerly side of the class line: Ain't nobody asked you to speak for us.

Of course there are external forces, economic and otherwise, that act on poor people and poor communities, and one of the intellectual failings of conservative social critics is our tendency to take those into considerably greater account in the case of struggling rural and small-town whites than in the case of struggling urban blacks. "Get off welfare and get a job!" has been replaced by solicitous talk about "globalization."

The reaction to the crack cocaine plague of the 1980s and 1990s was very different from the reaction to the opioid epidemic of the moment, in part because of who is involved—or perceived to be involved. In fact, this isn't the first time we've seen a rash of deaths from opioid overdoses. As Dr. Peter DeBlieux of University Medical Center in New Orleans put it, for a long time heroin addiction was treated in the same way AIDS was in its early days: as a problem for deviants. Nobody cared about AIDS when it was a problem for prostitutes, drug addicts, and those with excessively adventurous sex lives. The previous big epidemic of heroin overdoses involved largely non-white drug users. The current fentanyl-driven heroin episode and the growth of prescription-painkiller abuse involve more white users and more middle-class users.

But there are internal forces as well. People really do make decisions, and, whether they intend it or not, they contribute to the sometimes difficult conditions in which those decisions have to be made.

Consider the case of how I became homeless.

I wasn't homeless in the sense of sleeping in the park—most of the people we're talking about when we're talking about homelessness aren't. The people who are sleeping on the streets are mainly addicts and people with other severe mental-health issues. I was homeless by one Department of Health and Human Services definition: "an unstable or non permanent situation . . . forced to stay with a series of friends and/or extended family members." (As a matter of policy, these two kinds of homelessness should not be conflated, as they intentionally are by those who find it convenient, for political reasons, to pretend that our mental-health crisis is an economic problem.) Like many underclass families, mine lived very much paycheck to paycheck, and was always one setback away from economic catastrophe. That came when my mother, who for various reasons had a weakened immune system, got scratched by her poodle, Pepe, and nearly lost her right arm to the subsequent infection. A long hospitalization combined with fairly radical surgery and a series of skin grafts left her right arm and hand partially paralyzed, a serious problem for a woman who typed for a living. (She would later learn to type well over 100 words per minute with only partial use of her right hand; she was a Rachmaninoff of the IBM Selectric.) I am sure that there were severe financial stresses associated with her illness, but I ended up being shuffled around between various neighbors—strangers to me—for mainly non-economic reasons. My parents had two houses between them, but at that time had just gone through a very ugly divorce. My mother was living with a mentally disturbed alcoholic who'd had a hard time in Vietnam (and well before that, I am certain; his grandfather had once shot him in the ass with a load of rock salt for making unauthorized use of a watermelon from the family farm), and it was decided that it would be unsafe to leave children alone in his care, which it certainly would have been. He was very precise, in funny ways, and would stack his Coors Lite cans in perfect silver pyramids until he ran out of beer, at which point he would start drinking shots of Mexican vanilla, which is about 70 proof. Lubbock was a dry city then, and buying more booze would have meant a trip past the city limits, hence the resort to baking ingredients and, occasionally, to mouthwash. I am afraid the old realtors' trick of filling the house with the aroma of baked cookies has the opposite of the desired effect on me.

Our mortgage then was $285 a month, which was a little less than my father paid in child support, so housing was, in effect, paid for. And thus I found myself in the strange position of being temporarily without a home while rotating between neighbors within sight, about sixty feet away, of the paid-up house to which I could not safely return. I was in kindergarten at the time.

Capitalism didn't do that, and neither did illegal immigrants or Chinese competition with the Texas Instruments factory on the other side of town. Culture didn't do it, either, and neither did poverty: We had enough money to secure comfortable housing in a nice neighborhood with good schools. In the last years of her life, my mother asked me to help her sort out some financial issues, and I was shocked to learn how much money she and her fourth and final husband were earning: They had both ended their careers as government employees and had pretty decent pensions and excellent health benefits. They were, in fact, making about as much in retirement in Lubbock as I was making editing newspapers in Philadelphia. Of course, they were almost dead broke—their bingo and cigarette outlays alone were crushing, and they had bought a Cadillac and paid for it with a credit card.

They didn't suffer from bad luck or lack of opportunity. Bad decisions and basic human failure put them where they were. But that is from the political point of view an unsatisfactory answer, because it does not provide us with an external party (preferably a non-voting party) to blame. It was not the case that everything that was wrong with the lives of the people I grew up with was the result of their own choices, but neither was it the case that they were only leaves on the wind.

Of course, they were anti-elitists before it was fashionable, FDR Democrats who grew into Buchananism and Perotism before those became Trumpism. It might never have occurred to them to imitate the habits of people who had gone further and done better in life than they had, even though they had the experience of seeing people who came from the exact same conditions as they did—or, in some cases, from far worse circumstances—build happy, prosperous, stable, productive lives. My mother despised the college professors for whom she worked in her last job, who were unfailingly kind and generous to her, because they were unfailingly kind and generous to her, which she understood (as she understood many things) as condescension. Hers was a world of strict tribal hierarchy: She would, for example, enact petty cruelties on waitresses and grocery store clerks and other people in service positions, taking advantage of the fact that she had momentary social inferiors, and she must have been confused that the professors and deans did not behave that way toward her. In fact, they did the opposite, entrusting her with work far beyond her modest formal credentials or the official duties of her position. Class is funny in a small-ish town: The father of a school friend of mine became the dean of her college and her boss, and she spoke of the family as though they inhabited some faraway realm when in reality they lived three blocks north and two blocks east. That she herself could have had a life more like theirs, or that her children might yet, never occurred to her—it was sour grapes raised to a state of psychosis.

Feeding such people the lie that their problems are mainly external in origin—that they are the victims of scheming elites, immigrants, black welfare malingerers, superabundantly fecund Mexicans, capitalism with Chinese characteristics, Walmart, Wall Street, their neighbors—is the political equivalent of selling them heroin. (And I have no doubt that it is mostly done for the same reason.) It is an analgesic that is unhealthy even in small doses and disabling or lethal in large ones. The opposite message—that life is hard and unfair, that what is not necessarily your fault may yet be your problem, that you must act and bear responsibility for your actions—is what conservatism used to offer, before it became a white minstrel show. It is a sad spectacle, but I do have some hope that the current degraded state of the conservative movement will not last forever.

The thing about eternals truths is, they're eternal.

Dead Broke and Stone-Cold Stupid in Paradise

San Bernardino, California

O N THE FRONT DOOR OF THE SAN BERNARDINO CITY HALL is a sign that reads: "OUT OF ORDER." Broke city, broken door: There's a certain pleasing symmetry in the fact that the San Bernardino city council meets behind a door that, like the city government itself, does not work and is in urgent need of replacement. On this particular evening in late July, the council has met to make public what everybody already knows: Intellectually bankrupt, morally bankrupt—the city is under criminal investigation for sundry financial shenanigans—San Bernardino is above all old-fashioned bankrupt bankrupt, a pitiful penniless pauper that cannot even afford a cup of coffee. Seriously, the coffee guy wants cash up front now and has stopped serving the municipal office building until the city makes good on its latte liabilities. This is a paddle-free scato-riparian fiscal expedition of the first order.

After a great deal of self-congratulatory speechification—during which one council member used the phrase "the buck stops" no fewer than five times without once getting it quite right, laid out a little Boston Consulting–style two-by-two matrix to explain his analysis of the situation, repeatedly reminded the citizens of how often he had "prayed for strength" during his four long months in elected office, and

generally made a po-faced spectacle of himself—after all that, the feckless ladies and clueless gentlemen of the San Bernardino city council
voted to seek shelter under Chapter 9 of the U.S. bankruptcy code, a
law that deals specifically with municipal bankruptcies and grants cities
an extraordinary level of protection during financial reorganizations.
A phalanx of pant-suited she-bureaucrats and the city attorney
explained that in addition to filing for bankruptcy, the city needed to
declare a fiscal emergency, because it did not have enough money even
to last through the sixty-day waiting period that would follow initiating
the bankruptcy. The moment was not without levity: When one of the
ladies of the city council inquired as to which court would hear the
case, the city attorney explained that he was pretty sure the city's filing
under federal bankruptcy law would be heard in federal bankruptcy
court. When another council member inquired as to why the city was
filing under Chapter 9 instead of the more famous Chapter 11, the city
attorney gently explained that the municipality was filing under the
municipal-bankruptcy law because it is a municipality, not a guy with
hospital bills and a mortgage in default.

San Bernardino spends about 75 percent of its general-fund budget
on salaries, benefits, and pensions, with the vast majority of those
expenses coming from one class of employee: public-safety workers,
meaning cops and firemen, who earn as much as $230,000 a year with
overtime. Their pensions, as will not surprise anybody who has been
paying attention to government finances in recent years, are extraordinarily generous. In 2007, a consulting firm warned the city that its budget
was in trouble because its personnel costs were growing considerably
more quickly than its revenue, and the city's response was to . . . offer
even more generous pensions in the same year. The firemen are fat and
happy in the California sunshine, but the rest of San Bernardino is not
doing as well: "When times were good, my wife and I didn't go hog-wild
and play the let's-get-a-bigger-house game," says Mike Potter, who works
for a local construction firm. "But now times aren't good. At my company, 50 percent of the employees have been laid off, and I've taken a 15

percent pay cut. I was the head of engineering, and now I'm also a part-time receptionist and janitor." He is one of the lucky ones—the local unemployment rate runs around 15 percent—and he is blunt on the subject of what encumbers San Bernardino and other bankruptcy-bound California cities: "The public-employee unions are killing us. They are killing our cities, our states, and our country."

John Magness, the biggest real-estate developer in San Bernardino, is bearish on the city's near-term prospects. "No respectable developer would risk its relationships by getting its clients to locate in a city with this risk," he says. He estimates that his company's projects have added $1 billion to the city's tax base and about five thousand jobs over the past decade, but finds himself "reluctant to encourage customers to come here in this uncertain environment." He spoke in favor of the bankruptcy filing and fiscal emergency, arguing that they would give the city an opportunity to run a river of reform through the Augean stables of its finances, renegotiating contracts and rewriting the city charter. The local business leaders were nearly unanimous in endorsing the measures.

The citizens, as usual, were a mixed bag: One argued that the city's economic prospects could be turned around by recruiting a Trader Joe's to open, while another argued that the city's most pressing problem was the official harassment of "legitimate cannabis-based businesses." While a bottle of Trader Joe's Three-Buck Chuck and a few bong hits might take some of the sting out of the city's straits, its problems go much deeper. San Bernardino, like many California cities, like the state of California, and like the United States at large, is finding out the hard way that it is not as rich as it thought it was ten years ago. It's rich, of course—and California is fabulously rich—but it's like the rich guy who has taken out a $10 million mortgage on a house that turns out to be worth only $1 million: A million-dollar house is still a lot of house, but you have to make some adjustments. In 1999, at the peak of the dot-com stock market bubble, California reformulated its pensions and other public-employee-compensation practices, making them much, much more liberal than they had been. The state's Democrat-run legislature did this on the theory that pension investments would keep offering double-digit returns more or less forever, which led elected officials to make big promises and set aside approximately zilch to make good on them. If borrowing money to acquire an asset based on the theory that the appreciation of that asset will more than offset the cost of financing the borrowing sounds to you like the woeful tale of a million subprime mortgages, then they really could have used you in the California legislature a decade or so ago. In bubble after bubble after bubble, the country keeps repeating the practice that everybody swore off after the great market crash of 1929 and the Great Depression: investing on margin. California took out something very much like an adjustable-rate mortgage, financing present political consumption by in effect borrowing against future returns on the assets in its pension system—but the returns didn't materialize. CalPERS, the gigantic statewide pension system, was until a few weeks ago projecting 7.5 percent returns on its investments. Real returns: just over 1 percent. The entirety of the state's finances from top to bottom are exactly what one San Bernardino resident called his city's fiscal charade: a shell game.

In San Bernardino the results are pretty much in your face. Once a prosperous and well-scrubbed place, the city is now in such a sorry state that a local café owner at the meeting complained about the hookers tricking near her business. Vagrants are a source of constant complaints. San Bernardino is suffering from crime and slumification—more than a few residents suggested that if the city should need to make budget cuts, low-income housing programs are a good place to start. They pretty clearly would want them cut even if the city were absolutely flush—and it is widely remarked upon that many of the city's most influential businessmen no longer live in San Bernardino, having fled for well-heeled Rancho Cucamonga or other safe havens. With the locals getting gone, outsiders aren't eager to get into the real estate market. A developer described spending six years trying to recruit a Home Depot to open in the city. Whatever the orange-apron brigade's reservations about opening up shop in San Bernardino, available real estate surely was not among them. The Carousel Mall across from the city hall is one of those sprawl-ing two-story midcentury retail complexes, and it has a grand total of nine open shops. Most of the top floor is gated and shuttered, while the lower level has given up on retail entirely and converted the stores to office space. The garishly painted eponymous carousel is still and silent. On the upside, parking is a breeze.

While the city faces a great deal of trouble with its personnel costs, an even more toe-curling potential calamity awaits in the form of hun-dreds of millions of dollars of liabilities in economic-development grants, according to Warner Hodgdon, an astringent critic of the city govern-ment. The city offered the development concessions in the belief that the state would be picking up the tab, but Sacramento has some hairy fiscal problems of its own and is getting ready to leave San Bernardino and other cities twisting in the hot desert wind on those liabilities. Nobody seems to appreciate the irony that San Bernardino's economic future has been nuked by overambitious economic-development programs, and Hodgdon doubts whether the fiscal emergency and bankruptcy will be sufficient to deal with that problem. "I question whether this is a wise move," he said. "I spent ten years as chair of the economic-development agency. We were an all-American city, not all-American buffoons."

THE BUFFOONERY IS EPIDEMIC. Little places such as Mammoth Lakes have gone fiscally toes-up, as have bigger cities such as Vallejo. Bankrupt Stockton, one of the most dangerous cities in the country, has substantially reduced its police force, and signs of disorder are everywhere: garbage, police tape, vandalized properties. In the city's Garden Acres neighborhood—also known as "Okieville"—tattooed young men ape the style and mannerisms of Sinaloa gangsters. (I sup-pose it is possible that they *are* Sinaloa gangsters, middle managers dispatched to a branch office.) But like a lot of cities burdened with gigantic pension liabilities, Stockton is paying so many police so much not to police that it can't afford to pay police to police. Just outside Los Angeles, the city of Compton is probably bankruptcy-bound, too.

Compton, once synonymous with ghetto gangsterism, had been making something of a comeback, but like San Bernardino it grossly (and perhaps criminally) mismanaged its finances, shuffling money around from special-fund accounts to pay general-fund bills, leaving it with a looming deficit almost equal to its annual budget. Its bonds are junk, and its auditing firm, Mayer Hoffman McCann, was fined $300,000 for failing to detect irregularities leading up to a 2010 corruption scandal in Bell, California. And even that firm won't sign off on the city's current financials: It quit rather than publish an opinion on the statements, citing unresolved fraud allegations. Mayer Hoffman McCann: Straight outta Compton.

The bad news is that there are a lot of Comptons, Stocktons, and San Bernardinos out there. Los Angeles may prove to be one of them. The good news is that things have gone so sour that some California politicians have discovered that it hurts less to act than it does not to act. That is true at the municipal level but not yet true at the state level, which makes for some interesting mayors-versus-legislators politics.

"The enemy isn't Democrats or Republicans," says San Jose city councilman Sam Liccardo. "The enemy is *algebra*." Liccardo, a Democrat, is bracingly honest when it comes to his fellow partisans in Sacramento: "The fact is the unions own the Democratic Party," he says, and San Jose's pension-and-personnel reforms have not made the city's Democratic elected officials any friends in Sacramento. "Party orthodoxy is much more strictly enforced at the state level, because the unions decide who wins and who loses," Liccardo says. San Jose mayor Chuck Reed, also a Democrat, has been out front on the pension issue, and he's maybe had a little easier time with it than have the authorities in Compton or San Bernardino. His city is the capital of Silicon Valley, and his base of affluent Northern California professionals are not sending love letters to Paul Ryan, but they know how money works. "They may be liberal," he says, "but at some point you have to decide: Are we going to provide services or not?"

Reed has formed an unlikely partnership with the Republican mayor of San Diego, Jerry Sanders; the two authored letters to the legislature defending pension-reform efforts at the city level. "This isn't a partisan issue—66 percent of our citizens voted for the pension-reform initiative," Sanders says. "The state has been negligent, and a rift has broken out between the municipalities and the state." San Diego converted most of its pensions to a 401(k)-style plan, which, in addition to being more sustainable than a defined-benefit program, has the virtue of encouraging politicians to be prudent. "The employees can check their accounts," Sanders says, "so we have to make our contributions. They get to watch it grow." While San Diego is not entirely out of the woods—Sanders worries that a second national recession is on the horizon—the mayor is understandably proud of the fact that the city is projecting budget surpluses for the next five years. On the most critical issue facing California's struggling cities, he finds himself in agreement with his Democratic counterpart in San Jose: "Chuck is absolutely right."

CALIFORNIA IS A STATE with Hollywood at one end and Silicon Valley at the other, and driving along Route 1 between the two, you'd think its highways did nothing but connect money with money and success with success: From San Francisco's financial district down to Big Sur, from Beverly Hills to the solidly middle-class precincts of Orange County, California still is home to some of the richest, most productive, most energetic, and most creative people in the world, and watching the morning fog burn off of the Pacific, you can appreciate why every billionaire, rock star, and cult leader with any ambition at all makes his way to the Golden State. It's enough to make a Republican take up yoga. But there's another route between Los Angeles and San Francisco, too, through the blasted desert and agricultural backcountry. You don't have to get very far out of Los Angeles before you're in the world of "PIGS FOR SALE" signs, low-rent evangelical radio, and those millions of illegal aliens that Californians spend their time studiously not talking about. Unlike the wannabe Sinaloa bad boys up in Stockton, the backcountry farm boys have a sense of humor about Mexico's infamous syndicates: One produce-hauling entrepreneur moving a load of fresh tomatoes up Interstate 5 had the wit to call his carting business "CARTEL." He was running a big diesel, but in the more desolate corners of the state you wouldn't be too surprised to see a cart being pulled by oxen. It is sobering how empty, run-down, and poor much of interior California is. Bakersfield and environs are enough to make you wonder why the Joads even bothered: Tulsa is Paris by comparison.

San Jose and San Diego may be havens of relative fiscal sanity, but they are surrounded by Stocktons, Comptons, and San Bernardinos, along with the vast inland expanses that in many places have a disconcertingly Third World ambiance. Departing Los Angeles mayor Antonio Villaraigosa set many observers on edge when he talked about bankruptcy in connection with the city's fiscal future. "He says a bankruptcy won't happen under his watch," says Kevin James,[1] a Republican fiscal warrior running to replace him, "but his watch is over in a few months. He didn't say anything about what happens after that." The bankruptcy of the nation's second-largest city would not be a disaster in and of itself—it would only be San Bernardino writ large, a public confirmation of what everybody already knows.

Sinners in the Hands of an Indifferent God

New York, New York

THE GOD OF ABRAHAM is enigmatic, paradoxical, capricious, or so He must always seem to us, our understanding being imperfect, the limitations of our minds severe and unnegotiable. On Christmas we celebrate the fact that He, in His incomprehensible goodness, chose to dwell among us, for our salvation. Emmanuel, God Who Is With Us. The journey that begins in Bethlehem and ends (but does not end) at Golgotha must for our mortal days be the subject of faith—the reasoning mind recoils from it.

But there is another, less enigmatic, less mysterious god (capital letters are not his thing) who reminds us of his austere presence during these abbreviated days of winter: the god of passing time. New Year's is his Christmas, Lent, and Easter all at once, but he is undemanding when it comes to the rituals practiced in his honor. He requires no priest or intermediary. His law is inscribed not on our souls but on our cells. His church is every place where we are laid prone with our names written at our heads: every nursery ward, every graveyard. There is an old joke about two men who as newborns were laid side by side in the nursery, and who, at impossible odds, end up side by side in the same hospital room at the ends of their lives. One asks the other: "So, how was it for you?" You can make jokes about the god of passing time—he does not laugh, he is not offended, he is comprehensively indifferent, as cold and remote as the star over Bethlehem. If we make jokes about him, we make them for ourselves. The proverb tells us that the fear of the Lord is the beginning of wisdom. But nobody needs convincing when it comes to the god of passing time: We are born terrified of him and of the darkness of his eternal shadow. Winter is cold, and the ice is treacherous:

> To me belongeth vengeance and recompence;
> Their foot shall slide in due time:
> For the day of their calamity is at hand,
> And the things that shall come upon them make haste.

The first scuff on a nice new pair of shoes, or the first scratch in the paint of a new car, is a disappointment. You knew it was coming, but still the first one hurts. There are other scuffs and scratches soon enough. Every new pair of wingtips is destined to be a scuffed-up pair of old shoes, every new car is destined for the junk pile. But years are different: The first lost year hurts the least. Then they hurt more. Sometime around age thirty or so we approach a New Year's Eve, meditating on the year that is past, and think: "Well, didn't make much of that." We resolve to amend our ways. The ritual of the New Year is a peculiar one, a glass of champagne with a chaser of Puritanism, a supplementary Mardi Gras followed by a secular Ash Wednesday and a variable-length Lent for the casual unbeliever. A second scuff on the shoe, the locomotive of right-here-right-now dragging forward an ever-lengthening train of unre-formed years. But dragging it forward where? We resolve to amend our ways.

And the god of passing time draws nearer to us.

In Russia there is a Mount Yamantau, the name of which means "evil mountain." And perhaps it is an evil mountain—it is said to contain key elements of the Russians' "dead hand" nuclear-retaliation apparatus. There are other cursed mountains in the world, and there are sacred mountains. I once rode a rickety bus up narrow, back-bent mountain roads into the Himalayas and at the bottom of a gorge saw the irretrievable remains of an identical bus. I began to recall every time I'd written a headline reading "Bus Plunges into Ravine, XX Dead." That bus was the only place in India where I saw Hindus, Muslims, Sikhs, and Christians all praying together, fervently. Angels and ministers of grace defend us from gravity, that the driver's foot shall not slide. But the mountains were not evil mountains, or blessed mountains, or mountains of any moral inclination. They were mountains of unmindfulness. If the god of passing time has monuments, they are the mountains, built up and pulverized over eons. They are beautiful, and full of long-clawed, hungry things. It may be that all of us on that bus, Hindu, Muslim, Sikh, Christian, and terrified agnostic, were praying to the wrong deities.

With apologies to the Reverend Jonathan Edwards, we are sinners in the hands of an indifferent god. "Natural men's prudence and care to preserve their own lives, or the care of others to preserve them, don't secure 'em a moment. This divine providence and universal experience does also bear testimony to."

How dieth the wise man? As the fool.

But there is work to be done, and champagne to be had (in moderation—we resolve to amend our ways), and even though everybody—everybody—knows that everybody—everybody—at every—every—New Year's Eve party is only pretending to enjoy himself, we observe the proper offices and come together in our little pools of light in the brumal darkness.

And we may even raise a glass to the god of passing time, who is there, too. He is not unwelcome. He does not wish us ill.

He does not wish us anything at all.

Acknowledgments

The pieces in this book, selections from a decade of reporting, are published with the generous permission of my friends at *National Review*, the venerable magazine of politics and culture at which it has been my honor to work since 2008. The magazine's founder, William F. Buckley Jr., wrote often of the moral and civic necessity of gratitude, a virtue in which I have been at many times shamefully deficient. *National Review* permits me to go where I want, when I want, and write about what I want to write about the way I want to write about it—it is the best kind of job you can have in journalism. There are many people who help to make that work possible, among them *National Review* editor Rich Lowry, publisher Garrett Bewkes, National Review Institute president Lindsay Craig, and my friends at Regnery. John Podhoretz, Roger Kimball, Jason Lee Steorts, Charles C. W. Cooke, Rick Brookhiser, Ramesh Ponnuru, Katherine Howell, Jonah Goldberg, and the late Mike Potemra are a few among the many who have made my work better in direct and indirect ways, through their collaboration and their example as well as their friendship. But none of that could ever happen without the people who buy and read books, subscribe to magazines, and support the institutions that make this kind of work possible. My gratitude to these friends and colleagues is felt more often than it is expressed, and more strongly.

Full Copyright

Notes

Big White Ghetto

1. As of 2020, Owsley County had risen in the rankings and was only the third-poorest county in the United States, behind Wilcox County, Alabama, and Buffalo County, South Dakota. The former is a majority-black county that has seen some encouraging growth in jobs thanks to the presence of a Chinese-owned copper-tubing company, and the latter is taken up almost entirely by the Crow Creek Sioux reservation. So the folks in Owsley County are no longer the poorest people in America, but they remain the poorest white people in America.

White Trash Receptacle

1. Michael is today a much-valued colleague at *National Review*. Still pretty bitter.

"Boy"

1. In case you think this might be one of those Joe Biden "Cornpop" things, you can read about the exploits of Dumplin, real name Washington McCaskill, in the *New Orleans Times-Picayune*, November 9, 2017, and other editions. Matt Sledge, "Washington McCaskill, 3NG Gang Hitman Who Admitted Role in at Least 8 Killings, Gets 40-Year Sentence," *New Orleans Times-Picayune*, November 9, 2017, https://www.nola.com/article_b891e703-5f86-5757-aed9-eb47f8188a32.html.

Play to Extinction

1.   It tanked. After a series of bankruptcies and multiple owners, Revel sat empty for years. At one point, there was talk about putting up Syrian refugees there. In 2019, it was acquired by a New York City hedge fund, which operates it as Ocean Casino Resort. Governor Christie's hoped-for 14 percent increase in gambling revenue never materialized, and as of January 2018, revenue was in fact down almost 10 percent year over year. Governor Christie went on to be the biggest schmuck on the Trump transition team—no mean feat.

Topless Chick, Uncredited

1.   If her Twitter profile is to be believed, Nikki Phoenix is today a "Life, Health & Accident Insurance Agent."

Whose Streets?

1.   Later beaten by Antifa goons to the point of hospitalization.

Death of a Fucking Salesman

1.   Peggy Noonan, "Trump Is Woody Allen without the Humor," *Wall Street Journal*, July 27, 2017, https://www.wsj.com/articles/trump-is-woody-allen-without-the-humor-1501193193.

Pillars of Fire

1.   But not a coronavirus-control success story. Between the Saudi-Russian petro-price war and the crash in energy prices during the epidemic shutdown, the Midland unemployment rate shot up from 2 percent in December 2019 to 12.4 percent in May 2020. The line on the St. Louis Fed graph looks like a rocket taking off, and may prove very bad news indeed for a very long while in the Oil Patch.

In the Valley of the Giant Robots

1.   Pickens died peacefully in 2019; the Pickens plan died somewhat earlier and somewhat less peacefully. Pickens did not take criticism well, and grew so enraged by my pointing out the obviously self-serving nature of his proposal that I thought I was going to end up in a fistfight with the elderly gentleman right there in *National Review*'s editorial offices on the Upper East Side. He was, to say the very least, an American original.

The White Minstrel Show

1. Trump and his critics eventually came to resemble one another. When *National Review* ran its "Against Trump" cover, the response from the Trumpkins was a lot of sneering about how the magazine is losing money (which it has done since 1955) and subsidizes its operations with cruises and the like. (*National Review* was a pioneer in the magazine/nonprofit theme-cruise business.) In 2020, *National Review* ran a piece critical of the anti-Trump Lincoln Project, and Lincoln Project honcho Steve Schmidt responded as the Trumpkins did, almost verbatim: "*National Review* is basically insolvent and failing and its business model is sustained by hawking cruises." One of the true things that was said of the totalitarians of the twentieth century is that their great genius could be seen in how they caused their enemies to imitate them.

Dead Broke and Stone-Cold Stupid in Paradise

1. Not the actor.

Index

A

Abbott, Greg, 130–31, 133
abortion, 11, 22, 148
addiction, 10, 20, 33, 36, 39, 44–45, 48, 86–87, 97, 135, 203
addiction-treatment facilities, 43–44, 46
Adult Video News (AVN), 89, 93, 95, 97–99
AIDS, 41, 74, 78, 203
alcohol, 3, 9, 20, 22–23, 37, 59
Alcoholics Anonymous, 141
alcoholism, 20, 22, 44–45, 48, 196, 204
alt-right, the, 17, 119, 121–24, 126–27
American Conservative, the, 17, 123
Anglin, Andrew, 126–27

Antifa, 104–7
Appalachia, 1–3, 8, 11–13, 202
Atlantic City, 79–83, 85–86
Austin, 53, 129–37
authenticity, 197–98

B

bankruptcy, 199, 207–9, 211, 214
Barksdale, David, 62–65, 68–69
black men, 42, 195–96
Bloomberg, Mike, 7, 37
brothels, 90, 95–96
Buchanan, Pat, 25, 123, 144, 205
Burke, Edmund, 18–19, 27

C

California, 31, 38, 52, 80, 87, 92–93, 96, 109–15, 134, 145, 174, 197–98, 207–10, 212–14

capital, 6, 17–18, 21, 90, 163,
    178, 183
casinos, 39, 59, 77, 80–87, 90,
    96, 141, 159, 200
    taxes and, 82–83, 86
Charlottesville, 120, 127
China, 21, 40, 110, 145–46, 155–
    57, 160–62
Christie, Chris, 82–83
Clinton, Hillary, 112, 114, 143,
    146, 150
coal, 2, 5, 8, 11, 92, 178, 182,
    192–93
Colorado, 51–55, 58–60, 64, 167,
    182–83, 185–86
Compton, 211–12, 214
Confederates, 118–20
conservatism, 16–18, 25–26,
    121–23, 147, 196, 198, 206
consumerism, 90, 130
corn, 153–55, 160, 164
crime, 1, 6–8, 30, 37, 54, 59–60,
    62–64, 67, 71, 73, 76–77, 79,
    86, 93, 113, 210
Cruz, Ted, 20, 131–32
Cuomo, Andrew, 80, 84–85
CVS, 38, 42

D
DeBlieux, Peter, 40–42, 203
democracy, 105, 113, 122
Democratic Party, the, 105, 118,
    131, 143–44, 167, 212
diversity, 146
divorce, 22, 25–26, 45, 48, 127,
    134, 204
Dougherty, Mike, 16–18, 25

Dreher, Rod, 123
Drug Enforcement Administra-
    tion, 54
drugs, 7, 9, 38, 40, 60, 76
    cocaine, 18, 39–40, 63, 203
    heroin, 10, 20, 27, 35–37,
        39–49, 63, 130, 159, 203,
        206
    fentanyl, 35, 37, 40–41, 203
    marijuana, 51–60, 63
    opiates, 9, 33, 37–38, 159, 203
    oxy, 9, 38
    prescription painkillers, 9, 20,
        37–38

E
EBT funds, 6–7, 147
economy, the, 1, 6, 15–16, 18, 21,
    177, 183
elitism, 197, 199–200
engineers, 174–75, 181–84, 187,
    189–90, 192–93
environmentalism, 178, 182,
    185–90, 192–93
Environmental Protection Agency
    (EPA), 92, 178, 190, 193
European Union, 157, 162
eviction, 29–31

F
family, the, 15–16, 22, 26, 100
Farage, Nigel, 113
farmers, 19, 154–55, 157–64,
    188
farming, 11, 56, 153–55, 160–61,
    163–64
fascism, 105, 107, 121

FDA, 91–92
food stamps, 6–7
Fort, Jeff, 62–63, 68
Fracking, 173, 178, 183–87, 189–90, 192–93
Francis, Sam, 25–26
free speech, 118–20, 149
free trade, 121, 148, 155, 162, 177

G

gambling, 60, 77, 79–81, 83–87, 93
gangs, 39, 62–64, 66–68
gangsters, 60, 63–66, 211–12
Garbutt, 17–19, 25–27
Genting, 84–85
Giuliani, Rudy, 69, 77
Glenn, Sandra Dungee, 73–74
globalization, 22, 114, 127, 202
gun court, 74, 76–77

H

Hispanics, 19–20, 75
Mexicans, 19, 54, 68, 146, 206
homelessness, 43–45, 81, 130–33, 135–37, 203
Hoover, Larry, 62–65, 68

I

Ice-T, 195–96
identity politics, 123, 128, 150, 197
illegal immigration, 113–14, 146, 156, 204, 213
Immigration and Customs Enforcement (ICE), 102

infrastructure, 21, 113, 178, 183

J

jobs, 2, 6, 12, 21–22, 27, 33, 37, 112, 128, 135–37, 144–46, 149, 171, 174–76, 183, 190, 209

K

Kentucky, 1, 3, 5–7, 9–11, 13, 26, 39, 185
Kochs, the, 148–50
Kremlin, the, 106, 114–15

L

Las Vegas, 59, 92–93, 95, 99, 111
liberals, 10, 12, 62, 69, 76, 132, 149, 155, 212
libertarians, 9, 80, 114
Los Angeles, 62, 92–93, 113, 131, 211–14
low-income housing, 11, 61–62, 64, 68, 210

M

manufacturing, 22, 37
marriage, 10–11, 15, 22, 100, 111, 127
mental health, 135–36, 203
middle class, the, 72, 194, 203, 213
Minehart, Jeffrey, 74, 76
Mitchell, George, 189
monopolies, 80, 84
Moynihan, Daniel Patrick, 66

murder, 61–64, 69, 71–72, 74–77,
    84, 107, 127

N

national socialism, 144. *See also*
    socialism
nationalism, 16, 115, 145, 151.
    See also white nationalism
natural gas, 178, 182–83, 189–
    90, 193
Nazis, 119–20, 122–23, 125–26,
    201
Nebraska, 52–57, 60
New Orleans, 38–45, 203
New York City, 7, 17, 69, 84, 129,
    197–99
Ngo, Andy, 104–5
Nietzsche, 121–22
Nutter, Michael, 77

O

Obama, Barack, 67, 74, 145, 147,
    162, 177, 189–90, 197
oil, 37, 84, 144, 171, 173–80,
    182, 188–89, 192–93
Oregon, 112–13

P

Pennsylvania, 38, 80, 83–86,
    181–83, 185, 187–88, 190–92
pensions, 113, 205, 208–13
Philadelphia, 71–78, 85, 205
police, the, 64–65, 67–68, 73–75,
    77, 102–4, 106, 118, 120, 198,
    211
populism, 12, 199–201
pork industry, 156, 161

pornography, 89–100
Portland, 101–7
poverty, 1–2, 7–8, 10–11, 20–21,
    71, 201, 204
probation, 76
projects, the, 11, 61–62, 64–65,
    68–69
prostitution, 59–60, 95–96, 130,
    203
Purdue, 38–39

Q

QAnon, 167–68

R

race, 74, 123–24, 196, 201
rap music, 35, 195, 198
Rapoza, Terry, 113
Reagan, Ronald, 26, 101, 114,
    161, 195
refineries, 177–79, 192–93
regulation
    on drilling, 190, 193
    on drugs, 54, 58–59, 91
Rendell, Ed, 72, 77, 80, 185
rental properties, 31, 129, 135
Republican Party, the, 12, 17,
    105, 112, 121, 131, 150, 167,
    197, 200, 212

S

salesmen, 139–42
San Bernardino, 207–12, 214
sanctuary cities, 113
Sanders, Bernie, 111, 137, 143–
    50, 162, 168
Sanders, Jerry, 212–13

Scandinavia, 146, 148
Schwarzenegger, Arnold, 112
secession, 112, 114
Shakur, Tupac, 195
Social Security, 10, 17, 25, 79, 87
socialism, 134, 143–45, 151. *See also* national socialism
Soros, George, 149
Soviet Union, 20, 106, 110, 149
soybeans, 153–58, 160–61
Spencer, Richard, 119, 121, 123–24, 126–28
Street, John, 72–74, 77–78

T
tariffs, 154, 157, 163
taxes, 17–18, 32, 54, 68, 72, 93, 110, 113–14, 121–22, 136, 190, 209
technology, 94–95, 153, 160, 189, 192–93
trade, 145–46, 150, 154–57, 159, 161–62
trade deficits, 145–46, 156, 182
Trump, Donald, 12, 18–21, 25–27, 105, 111–14, 121–22, 131–32, 141–42, 150, 154–57, 160, 162, 167, 169, 197–202, 205

U
underclass, the, 8, 11, 29, 135, 196, 199, 201, 203
white, 27, 198, 201–2
unions, 72, 77, 106, 143–44, 209, 212

United Auto Workers (UAW), 143–44, 146
United Nations, 168

W
Walgreens, 36–40, 42
Washington, D.C., 17, 75, 110, 112, 131, 153, 156, 162, 164, 167
wastewater, 178, 186–87, 191, 193
welfare, 4, 8, 10–11, 19, 21, 79, 87, 114, 136, 146, 148, 202, 206
Wheeler, Ted, 103–4
white nationalism, 25, 120–23, 125–27
white supremacy, 104, 122, 124
white working class, 1, 17–19, 26, 37, 42, 197–98
World Trade Organization, 162

Y
Yes California, 109–10, 112–14